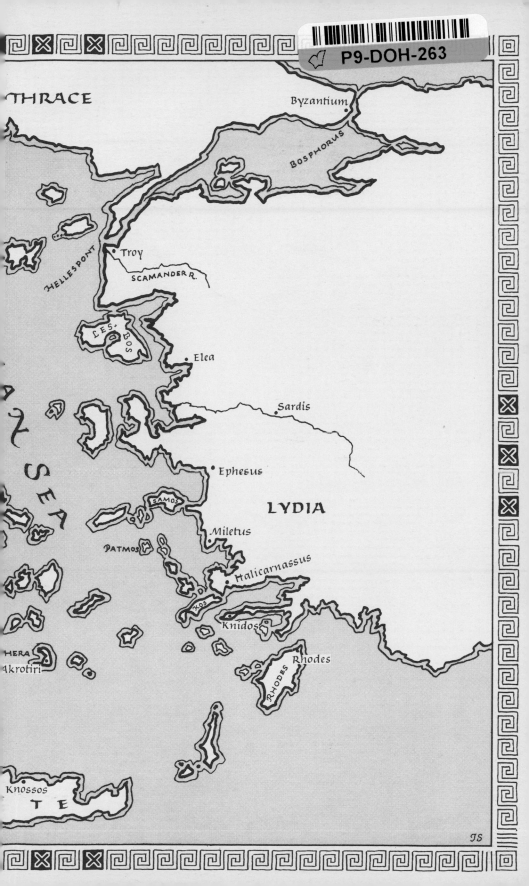

THRACE

Byzantium

BOSPHORUS

HELLESPONT

Troy

SCAMANDER R.

LES-
BOS

Elea

Sardis

Ephesus

LYDIA

SAMOS

Miletus

PATMOS

Halicarnassus

KOS

Knidos

HERA

Rhodes

RHODES

Akrotiri

AN SEA

Knossos

TE

JS

ALPHA TO OMEGA

BOOKS BY

ALEXANDER AND NICHOLAS HUMEZ

Latin for People / Latina pro Populo

The Boston Basin Bicycle Book

(WITH EDWARD AND JANICE GOLDFRANK)

ALPHA
TO
OMEGA

The Life & Times
of the Greek
Alphabet

Alexander &
Nicholas Humez

David R. Godine · Publisher
BOSTON

First published in 1981 by David R. Godine, Publisher, Inc.

306 Dartmouth Street, Boston, Massachusetts 02116

Library of Congress Cataloging in Publication Data
Humez, Alexander.   alpha to omega.
Includes index.
1. Greek language—Alphabet.
I. Humez, Nicholas D., joint author.   II. Title.
PA273.H8   481′1   80-83955
ISBN 0-87923-377-X

Printed in the United States of America

For Louie Howland who put us up to it.

Contents

Prologue

This is a book about the Greek alphabet, about ancient Greek culture, and what these have given us. "Ancient Greece" to most readers will perhaps conjure up a tableau of Athens in the fifth century B.C., of Socrates, Alcibiades, Euripides, Pheidias, Pericles, and Aristophanes set against a dazzling backdrop of the Acropolis in all its glory, sandwiched in time between the last Persian invasion and the outbreak of the Peloponnesian War. We *will* talk about that time and space in Greek life, to be sure; but there is a great deal more to Greek civilization than that. Greeks lived in *all* the lands on the coast of the Aegean Sea, including western Asia Minor; had colonies flourishing as far off as Sicily and the French Riviera; and were firmly ensconced in southern Italy – it is not for nothing that the Romans called this land *Magna Graecia*, "Great(er) Greece." Moreover, thanks to the conquests of Alexander the Great, Palestine and Egypt saw rule by Greek kings until the Romans came; and Alexandria, at the mouth of the Nile, boasted the best library in antiquity and rivaled even Athens as a center of learning. And Byzantium, which Constantine made the seat of the eastern half of the Roman empire, survived the fall of Rome to the barbarians by a thousand years, shining as a beacon of learning and high culture through Europe's darkest ages.

Nor did the golden age of Greece spring full-grown from Chaos. Antedating fifth-century Athens was a millennium of Greek civilization, beginning with the probably non-Greek Minoans, based largely on Crete, from whom the succeeding Mycenaean Greeks liberally borrowed as they extended their power throughout the Peloponnese. (It was the Mycenaeans who fought in the

Trojan War and their successors who carried the banner of Greek civilization forward to the fifth century B.C.) In turn, other nations borrowed heavily from the Greeks, to our good fortune: We are indebted to the Romans and the Arabs for preserving much of what we now know of the Greeks and their multifarious contributions to literature and learning. Thus, to talk of the ancient Greeks is of necessity to talk of the mysterious Minoans, the Egyptians, Persians, Phoenicians, Romans, Jews, Arabs, and Vikings, among others – people who contributed to Greek culture, drew from it, or (as so often happened) both.

If the whole of ancient Greek culture properly covers a spread of several thousand years and an area including at least the whole of the Mediterranean Sea and coastlands, we may be pardoned for approaching the subject with a scattergun technique: There is simply so much to it that one can't possibly hope to cover more than a modest fraction in a lifetime, let alone in a single book, save by spotlighting particular places and times to the near exclusion of others. Fortunately, an abecedarian book is well suited to just this sort of selective sample: a series of glimpses of the Greek world and its impact on our own – historical, philosophical, mathematical, cosmological, rhetorical, political.

The reader may have noted that the last six words are themselves of Greek origin. This is no coincidence: We owe these *concepts* to the Greeks as well. The words we use define our world view and shape it at the same time. Anyone who uses a word derived from Greek is, to a very large extent, *thinking* like a Greek, consciously or not. The vocabulary of a language is a mirror of the lives of its speakers; its subsets of words borrowed from other languages represent clusters of ideas borrowed from those other cultures. The Greek borrowings present in English vocabulary are distinct borrowings from the Greek world view as well.

Our book is divided into twenty-four sections, one for

each letter of the Greek alphabet; the accompanying narratives look at English words – some common, some esoteric, all legitimate and current – that come from Greek words beginning with the letter at hand and explore the aspects of Greek culture behind the borrowed words. A twenty-fifth section rounds out the alphabet by examining the "lost" letters – those which were once part of the Greek alphabet but were later discarded as superfluous. In all this we shall do our best to convey at least a whiff of the atmosphere of ancient Greece and a sense of what it meant to be touched by things Greek; for the reader whose appetite has been whetted, there is a selective bibliography at the end of the book suggesting where to look for more – and there is *always* more.

A Note on Transliteration

All of the Greek words cited in the following pages are given, not in the Greek orthography (with which the reader may not be thoroughly familiar until after having read the book from cover to cover), but in the more readily accessible Roman script that we use for writing in English. For those who might be curious to find out more about the cited words by checking in a Greek-English dictionary or might simply wish to see how the words look in Greek script, we offer the following system of transliteration, which we have employed throughout.

Greek		Roman	Greek		Roman
Aα	alpha	a	Nν	nu	n
Bβ	beta	b	Ξξ	ksi	ks, (x)
Γγ	gamma	g; n (before g, k, and ch)	Oo	omicron	o
			Ππ	pi	p
Δδ	delta	d	[ϙ	koppa	q, k]
Eε	epsilon	e	Pρ	rho	rh
[F	vau, digamma	w]	Σσ s	sigma	s
Zζ	zeta	z	Tτ	tau	t
Hη	eta	ē	Yυ	upsilon	y, (u)
Θϑ	theta	th	Φφ	phi	ph
Iι	iota	i	Xχ	chi	ch
Kκ	kappa	k, (c)	Ψψ	psi	ps
Λλ	lambda	l	Ωω	omega	ō
Mμ	mu	m	[ϡ	sampi	-----]

The three Greek orthographic signs given here in brackets – *vau* (*digamma*), *koppa*, and *sampi* – do not appear in the standard Greek alphabet, though all were used at one time or another in Greek writings. *Vau* (*digamma*) appeared in early Greek versions of the alphabet between *epsilon* and *zeta* and had the phonetic value of Modern English *w*. This letter underlies the Roman letter *f*. *Koppa* appeared in early Greek versions of the alphabet between *pi* and *rho* and had the phonetic value of our *k*. It forms the basis of the Roman letter *q*. *Sampi* (a combination of the Phoenician letter *san* and the Greek letter *pi*) was never assigned a position in the alphabet but was nonetheless used in the Greeks' alphabetical system of mathematical notation. All three of these letters are discussed in the final chapter of this book.

The alternate Roman transliterations given here in parentheses – *c* for *kappa*, *x* for *ksi*, and *u* for *upsilon* – are conventional in English and appear in this book in the rendering of Greek words in which *k*, *ks*, or *y* would seem unnecessarily pedantic or misleading. Greek words cited in the text appear with their now-conventional accents: acute (´), grave (`), and circumflex (^). Accent was not marked in the Greek orthography before about 200 B.C. when the Alexandrian librarian, Aristophanes of Byzantium, is said to have introduced the practice. Originally, Greek had a system of tonal or pitch accentuation somewhat like that of Modern Chinese. This eventually shifted to a system of stress accentuation, comparable to that of Modern English. Aristophanes of Byzantium (or some other happy culprit) seems to have happened along at a point after the tone-to-stress shift was a fait accompli, so it is not altogether clear just what the "modern" orthographic accents represented when it comes to a question of the pronunciation of Ancient Greek. Suffice it to say that the circumflex appears only over long vowels and the grave over short vowels in the

ALPHA TO OMEGA

◄ A ►

ALPHA

IS FOR *ALPHABET*, ARGUABLY THE SIN-
gle most influential and far-reaching of humankind's
many ingenious inventions to date. The word "alphabet"
comes from the names of the first two letters of the
Greek alphabet, *alpha* and *beta*, run together and left to
stand for the whole shebang, much in the way that we
speak of knowing our ABCs when we mean the complete
set of orthographic signs that we use to represent the
English language. (A similar convention is found in
Urdu, which is written in Arabic script; the word for a
person who is just beginning to learn to read and write is
abjad-khvān – a[*lif*], b[*ē*], j[*im*], and d[*al*] being the first
four letters of their almost-alphabet in their original
order, first cousins to Greek *alpha, beta, gamma,* and
delta.) The expression "*alpha* to *omega*," like our own
"A to Z," perhaps the more logical candidate for naming
the alphabetical array, was reserved early on for grander
purposes, namely, to characterize *anything* whole, complete, or exhaustive for which the alphabet itself provided an apt and readily accessible metaphor.

So, where did the alphabet come from and where has
it gone? And what do we mean by "*the* alphabet" anyway? The story starts, according to latest accounts, some
11,000 years ago in Mesopotamia (literally, "in the middle of – between – the rivers"), the region between the
Tigris and Euphrates so aptly named the Fertile Crescent. As it now seems, thanks largely to the pioneering
research of Denise Schmandt-Besserat, the traders of that
early time and place evolved the practice of sending
primitive bills of lading along with their goods – cows,
bales of hay, or what have you – to insure that nothing
would fall by the wayside in the transmission of the lot

from merchant A to merchant B. These "invoices" apparently took the form of sealed earthenware jars containing stylized tokens for each item of commerce being sent and received, which was all very well if it was just a case of merchant A commissioning teamster B to haul a load of goods to merchant C. However, with the advent of jobbers and brokers and wheelers and dealers of every stripe, a more sophisticated method of record keeping became necessary to insure that if there was perchance any "inventory shrinkage" between the original sender and ultimate recipient of the merchandise, the point of ripping-off could be easily ascertained. Thus, a system of marking the outside of the sealed jar was invented. From these outside markings, the middlemen could see whether or not they had received all of the promised goods without having to break open the jar that contained the original sender's tokens. From these markings – the stylized renderings of the stylized tokens inside the jars – is thought to have evolved a pictographic system of writing eagerly adopted by the various peoples of the Near East.

Pictographic writing, that is, a system of representing speech through the use of pictures, was a great idea, but one with certain limitations. There are, after all, plenty of things to talk about that don't readily lend themselves to pictographic representation, and, as any parent who has ever been asked to interpret his or her child's early artwork will attest, one person's ibis is another's crane or elephant or Uncle Joe. Clearly, to make such a system work, would-be readers and writers must agree on a large inventory of stylized, readily reproducible symbols, many of which will inevitably have little or nothing to do, as pictures, with what they were chosen to represent. And indeed, it was not too long before the vast majority of the consensual signs of early Near Eastern orthography took on a wholly arbitrary, nonrepresentational cast, becoming utterly indecipherable to all but the professional initiates to the art of writing. This was great if you were a career scribe, but not so fine if you were a bricklayer who wanted to be able to read the sports page or the graffiti on the walls of the local bordello without having to go to graduate school.

Eventually, some clever soul – or, much more likely, a consortium of clever souls – hit on the idea that reading and writing would be a lot simpler if, instead of representing individual words and grammatical constructions, the orthography could be geared to the phonetics of the language in question. Languages make do with a relatively small number of contrasting sounds as the basic building blocks for their words, and it would obviously be more economical to represent these recurrent elements by written symbols than by different symbols for each word. As a first approximation, different written symbols were used to represent different syllables in the various languages of the Near East. (This is something of an over-simplification, since at first there was a mix of the old with the new – some symbols still stood for words while others stood for phonetic entities of syllable length – and, since the languages in question didn't always have the same syllabic structure, some backing and filling was required to make the writing system work properly in each case. But no matter: It was all in a few thousand years' work.) The system eventually refined itself to the point that the literate locals of the Fertile Crescent and their immediate neighbors came to represent the various consonantal sounds of their languages by individual letters, much as the speaker-reader-writers of the modern Semitic languages – notably Arabic and Hebrew – do today. The vowel sounds were left unwritten for some reason, a practice maintained to this day in the Arabic and Hebrew scripts, which either make no mention of vowels or else represent them with diacritical marks of one sort or another.

It is at this point in the eighth or ninth century B.C. that the Greeks enter the picture, borrowing the latest version of the Near Eastern almost-alphabetical writing system and making certain improvements on it in fairly short order. Tradition has it that the raw material for the Greek alphabet was brought to Boeotia by a Phoenician named Kadmos (Cadmus). Kadmos was said to have been the son of the Phoenician king Agenor, and the brother of Europa – whom Zeus set out to seduce, appearing to her in the form of a bull, and whom he eventually carried off. Agenor sent Kadmos off in search of Europa. Having had no luck in finding his sister, Kadmos went to consult the Delphic oracle who told him that he should follow a wandering cow and establish a city wherever she might stop to graze, which he did, and there the Boeotian city of Thebes was established. (One is reminded of the traditional explanation given for the bizarre layout of the winding streets of Boston, namely, that the colonials turned their cows loose to wander as they pleased, and wherever they wandered, a street was defined for future generations.) Kadmos is said to have brought sixteen letters with him to give to the Greeks, who are said to have added another ten (of which two subsequently fell into disuse), thus bringing the inventory up to the standard twenty-four. Why Kadmos chose to give the Greeks only sixteen of the twenty-two letters of the Phoenician protoalphabet is not clear, but then most legends have cracks in them large enough to accommodate as much history and logic as anyone could ask to slip between them, so who are we to quibble over a few chicken scratches?

Besides, the story of Kadmos does have a grain of probable historical truth to it: The Greeks *did* apparently borrow the basics for their alphabet – or alphabets, since until the fourth century B.C. or so, several closely related alphabetic scripts were in use in the Greek-speaking world – from those adventurous sea-going entrepreneurs, the Phoenicians, at some point during the eighth or possibly ninth century B.C. The rest of the tale of Kadmos and the alphabet may be taken with a grain of salt. The Phoenician alphabet seems to have been borrowed pretty much lock, stock, and barrel, and Boeotia was probably not the first Greek-speaking region in which this borrowing took place.

Actually, it would appear that the inchoate alphabet first reached Crete and the Aegean Islands and was later wafted over the waters to mainland Greece on the local trade winds. One or two earlier local attempts to evolve a reasonable writing system seem to have followed this same maritime course: The syllabic scripts of Minoan Linear A – as yet undeciphered – and Linear B, the orthographic embodiment of the language of the Mycenaean empire of the fifteenth to thirteenth centuries B.C., first made their appearance on Crete, whether as native inventions or as tinkered-with borrowings from the Near Eastern mainland. (Scholars hedge, having so far failed to make sense of Linear A, about the language that its users might have spoken, though it is now clear that the Mycenaean writers of Linear B spoke an early dialect of Greek.) Both Linear A and Linear B fell into disuse, however, before they had a chance to really flex their muscles.

Several dialects of Greek, then, made the Phoenician script their own, with a few additions, deletions, and authors' alterations. This was to be expected, since the sounds of Phoenician and the sounds of Greek did not by any means correspond one to one – for openers, Greek is an Indo-European language and Phoenician is (or was) Semitic – and, besides, the Greeks thought it would be an improvement to represent the vowels as well as the consonants of their language, something which apparently had not occurred to the Phoenicians. The upshot of it all was that one set of Greeks worked out a fairly coherent alphabet, which has subsequently been dubbed Western Greek and which was the first-draft form passed on to the Etruscans who then passed it on to the Romans who then passed it on to us. Another group – the so-called Eastern Greeks – developed another, which eventually became the alphabet of Classical (Attic-Ionic) Greek, the script in which most of the many great monuments to Greek reason and fancy were first written down for posterity. And as far as posterity is concerned, if you read a modern-day publication in Greek, it will be in "eastern" script, and if you read Russian, it will be in a script derived from that (with some adjustments, of course).

So then what happened? The literate members of the Greek population wrote and read alphabetically, but this was not all. The letters of the alphabet soon took on another function or two, being as handy as they were. First, as had been so with the Semitic letters, the elements of the Greek alphabet found themselves being used as a primitive though by no means unsophisticated form of mathematical notation: Different letters and combinations of letters stood for different numbers. A second innovation was the use of the letters of the alphabet in musical notation. The Greeks worked out two systems for writing music down, each based on the alphabet or its adjuncts. The first, primarily for the preservation of instrumental music on paper, involved the use of purely alphabetical symbols (a few of which may have been retained for the purpose from scripts of the Near East); and the second, primarily for vocal music, made extensive use of the accent marks – grave, acute, and circumflex – to mark rising, falling, and rising-falling musical tones. It is this latter system which underlies our modern-day method of musical notation.

The other ramifications of alphabetic writing are so numerous and so profound that we could not possibly do them justice in this single chapter about *alpha*, the first and foremost, nor perhaps in the course of this whole book, though we will give it a whack. The alphabet was an invention staggering in its implications. And there is some truth to the old wheeze that it was only invented once, which makes it all the more remarkable. In the pages that follow, we will try to give some sense of what the Greeks did with this singular contribution to humankind, hitting on as many of the high points as we can of the stuff that they chose to express in the medium of print. Read it in good health, and thank the Greeks.

◄ B ►

BETA

IS FOR *BOUSTROPHEDON*. BOUSTRO-
phedon means "as the ox plows," that is, back and forth,
back and forth, alternating right to left and left to right,
or vice versa. This is, of course, the sensible way to plow
a field with an ox: It would be unthinkable, after all, to
walk your beast of burden back the whole length of the
field just to start the next furrow on the same side as the
last. (An extension of this logic led the English early on
to favor long and thin plots of farm land – an acre was
originally the amount of land that you and your ox could
plow in a day. If your land was long and thin, you lost
less time getting the ox around the turns.) What, then,
could be more natural to the ancients in their basically
agrarian world than to look upon the written representation of speech as simply another sort of furrowing of
virgin soil, left to right, right to left, then left to right,
and so on in a continuous line of letters rounding each
corner of print on the page without ever breaking the
flow of the message?

This sort of writing, known as *boustrophedon*, was
widely practiced by the early Greeks. They had received
the alphabet from their neighbors in the Near East without any clear instructions as to how the letters should
best be oriented on the page and so were obliged to sort
this out for themselves, which they did after experiment-
ing with both right-to-left, left-to-right, and boustrophedon scripts.

Nowadays, of course, we tend to take for granted the
orientation of both the individual letters and lines of
letters on a page, but each presents its own problems, as
the skewed writing of the child and the reversals of the
dyslexic both testify. It is said that the origin of the

expression "mind your *p*'s and *q*'s" lies with the advent of movable type and the master printer's often-felt need to admonish the apprentice (or printer's devil) to keep these two letters apart. (Another etymology has it that the *p* stood for "pint" and the *q* stood for "quart" in the medieval alehouse, and you had better not get so utterly blotto that you wouldn't catch the proprietor writing down a *q* on the tab when you had in fact only been served a *p*.) The Greeks did not have to grapple with this sort of thing: Their alphabet contains *no* letters that, when rotated on the vertical or horizontal axis, look like any others in the alphabet. And in fact, a surprising number of the letters of the Greek alphabet are symmetrical (more often than not along their vertical axis).

It was evidently sufficient unto the ancient Greek day to get the message down on paper in *some* kind of order: If the message about-faced every other line, that was of no great consequence. By about 300 B.C., with the virtually pan-Greek adoption of the left-to-right Ionic script, some semblance of order had been introduced into the writing system, and by the time of the Roman Empire, the demands of bureaucratic efficiency had stabilized writing into the familiar left-to-right, top-to-bottom system that we now all know and love: Very few classical Greek or Roman inscriptions read anything other than strictly left to right, top to bottom.

This is not to say that left-to-right, top-to-bottom writing is intrinsically superior to right-to-left or columnar script. Hebrew and Arabic read right to left, and traditional Chinese script and its derivatives read top to bottom, right to left (although the exigencies of the publishing, printing, and binding industries with their Western-made machinery, and, in scientific writing, the awkwardness of rendering Latinate names and numbers vertically have caused a shift in the Oriental scripts to Roman orientation). Besides, readers seem to be fairly tolerant of at least some reorientations of the literary line, though nobody, apparently, likes to read from the bottom of the page to the top. (Western printers, back in the hot-metal days, used to read beds of type upside down and backwards, the top line to be printed winding up the bottom line as the printer looked at it, but nobody ever said that they *liked* it.) But other orthographic aberrations are routinely taken in stride: Almost all literate cultures have by now had to deal with the reorientation of shop signs from horizontal to vertical as the population has grown and the competition for visual space on the street has become more fierce.

Speakers of Hindi, whose script is semisyllabic and does not lend itself readily to alphabetic segmentation, prefer to write the letters on their signs smaller in order to have the words on them still read left to right without a break. Users of other writing systems have been more adventurous. In the case of the ancient Greeks, shop signs seem to have been largely emblematic, without inscription: A jug for a tavern called *The Amphora*, and so forth. At Pompeii, the remains still stand of a brothel whose outer wall was painted with lewd frescoes so that even the illiterate might not mistake the nature of the establishment; though it seems also to have been the custom in Magna Graecia for those patrons who *were* literate to deface the wall with obscene graffiti, just to strut their stuff.

Muslims writing in Arabic script, on the other hand, have raised the art of sign painting to a degree unparalleled anywhere else in the Western world. Prohibited by the Koran against pictorial representation for fear of idolatry, the Arabs developed the calligraphy of signs and inscriptions as a separate art form, called *tughra*. The move from right-to-left horizontal signs to accommodation to the vertical was considered a challenge. Only in ancient China, where it is said to have ranked above painting, has calligraphy held such high status.

But back to *boustrophedon*, a compound whose first component part is *boû(s)*, "ox." This noble beast seems to have been domesticated and bred long before the

Greeks. Remains of already specialized breeds of cattle have been dated in both India and Mesopotamia to 4000 B.C. The parent stock of most domestic breeds is now generally held to have been the aurochs, a hefty (800–1000 kg) beast with curved horns and an extremely feisty disposition. The slow, methodical temper that we think of as the essence of bovinity is the result of millennia of breeding. The domestic cattle of the Greeks were much more spirited creatures, some of them perhaps no more than a generation or two from the wild ox. Wall paintings in Crete, for example, show acrobats literally taking the bull by the horns and executing handsprings, powered in large measure by a shake of the mighty animal's head. A specialized strain of fighting bull, easily excitable and retaining a slightly foreshortened version of the curved horn, is still favored by the Spanish for use in the bull ring.

The last aurochs on record died an elderly cow in Poland in 1627, despite belated, though nonetheless determined, government efforts to save the herd, which was down to thirty-eight head in 1564. Although provided with the services of several game wardens, the run of the sovereign's private woods at Jaktorow, and extra rations of hay to make it through the winter, by 1599 the herd had shrunk to twenty-four, and all but the last of that number were dead twenty-five years later. The last portrait of an aurochs from life, a painting on wood by an anonymous sixteenth-century artist, surfaced in an antique shop in Augsburg some two hundred years later. It was bought and reproduced in black and white by the English zoologist Hamilton Smith for publication in 1827. The *earliest* known portrait of an aurochs is undoubtedly the one on the cave wall at Lascaux, where it appears with one of its next of kin, the bison. It is not clear why the aurochs was domesticated and the bison was not.

Strophé, the second major member of the word *boustrophedon*, was the name given to the sally from one side of the stage to the other of the Greek chorus in classical theater, and thus to the choral number that they sang while doing this. The return trip across the stage, when the verse was sung, was called the *antistrophé*. Both *strophé* and *antistrophé* are derived from the verb *stréphein*, "to turn." (The word *verse* is derived from the Latin verb *vertere*, which also means "to turn.") Thus, *boustrophedon* literally means something on the order of "the ox having made his turn." *Bucolic* ("rustic") comes directly from *boukolikós*, the adjective formed from *boukólos* ("herdsman"). The Romans used this word as an epithet for a type of pastoral poetry, and as a contemptuous term for a country bumpkin. *Bulimia* (from *boûs* and *limós*, "hunger") is a pathological state in which the victim suffers from an intense craving for food, the idea being, presumably, that one has the appetite of an ox. *Boondocks* does not, alas, derive from *boûs*. Rather, it is U.S. Army slang from the Pacific Theatre of World War II: Its source is the Tagalog word *bundok*, meaning "mountain" or "hinterland."

Ββ

13

◂ Γ ▸

GAMMA

IS FOR *GAIA, GENESIS, GAMETE,* AND
gynecology, words that the Greeks themselves might
have considered as something of a boxed set, since each
has something to do with procreation and the family,
and women's crucial, if not wholly enviable, role therein.

Gaia is the original Earth Mother in the Greek cosmology, *gē* (*géa*) being the standard Greek word for
"earth." Gaia was said to have sprung from the primal
Chaos, more or less under her own steam, and to have
single-handedly produced her son and mate, Ouranos
(the sky), bearing several children by him before de-
ciding he was more trouble than he was worth. These
children – the Titans, the Cyclopes, and the Hekatoncheires – provided, with a little further help and encouragement from Gaia, the stock from which the rest of the
extended, incestuous family of the Greek gods were
generated. Gaia's help and encouragement took many
forms, including a willingness to mate with her grandson,
Poseidon, to produce the giant Antaeus, who, as an
adult, ingenuously offered to wrestle Herakles (Hercules)
to the death. The latter soon realized that whenever
Antaeus took a fall and came in contact with the earth,
he was replenished and refortified; so Herakles simply
throttled his adversary while holding him up in the air.

Genesis means "birth" and comes from the root that
underlies the verb *gígnesthai,* "to be born," the mediopassive form of the verb meaning "to beget, produce,"
with its many cognates in the other Indo-European
languages. English for its own part has *kin, kind, king,*
and *kindergarten* from its Germanic heritage, as well as
a host of Greco-Latin derivatives. From Latin, we get
genus, the intervening taxonomic class between the fam-

ily and the species; *genitals* and *progeny*, and *generation* and *general* (which originally meant "specific," that is, "pertaining to a species, type, or *genus*"). Greek, not to be outdone, supplies us with such worthies as *Eugene* – Russian *Yevgeny* – "well-born"; *genesis*, as in the name of the first book of the Old Testament, and the term *parthenogenesis* ("virgin birth"), a commoner phenomenon in the ancient world than one might guess. Science has appropriated *genetics*, *genes*, and the *-gen* of *hydrogen*, ("water-producer," because when combined with *oxygen* it produces water); *carcinogen* ("cancer-producer"); and *antigen*, the generic term for any foreign body whose introduction into the blood stream results in the generation of antibodies to fight it off.

Greek *gámos* meant "marriage," a *gametés* being a husband and a *gameté* being a wife. In English, a *gamete* is a cell capable of reproduction when paired with its opposite number, egg or sperm. The Greek *-gam-* of sociosexual union is also found in the words *monogamy* (marriage to one person – at least at a time), *polygamy* (marriage to more than one person at a time), and the Late Latin hybrid, *bigamy* (marriage to two people at the same time). Why the Romans felt it necessary to coin a term for this latter variety of multiple marriage is not at all clear, though perhaps it was the only kind that ever got brought to court in their fundamentally monogamous society.

A note about the *-gam-* words: Dorothy Parker's clever double dactyls imputing a penchant toward monogamy to women and polygamy to men ("Hogamus, higamus/ Man is polygamous/Higamus, hogamus/Woman's monogamous") notwithstanding, *gamete* and the *-gamy*s are quite neutral as to the sex of their referents. "Spouse" would actually have been a more accurate gloss for both *gametés* and *gameté*: A woman can have two husbands and a man can have two wives, and it will still be *bigamy* – or *polygamy*, if anyone prefers. If, our prurient interests readily aroused, we wish to disambiguate a polygamous relationship, we can call a woman with more than one husband *polyandrous* and a man with more than one wife *polygynous*. These are, of course, by no means the only or the most colorful epithets that our own basically monogamous society eagerly attaches to the bigamist, or "two-timer," but their meanings are clear and their pedigree is respectable Greek. *Polyandrous* derives from *polý*, "many" and *anér/andrós*, "man"; and *polygynous* derives from *polý*, "many" and *gyné/gynaikós*, "woman."

Anér/andrós was only one of the Greek words that we translate as "man." As Liddell and Scott put it at the turn of the century, *anér* was "man as opposed to woman," glossing *ánthrōpos* as "man as opposed to beast," i.e., a human being of either sex. It is *ánthrōpos* that gives us *misanthrope* and *anthropology*, "hater of mankind" and "study of mankind," respectively. (Note that while there are special terms in English for haters of women and students of womankind – "misogynists" and "gynecologists," respectively – there are no such terms for haters of members of the male sex or students of maleness.) *Ánthrōpos* also gives us *anthropomorphism*, that thoroughly human tendency to ascribe human form and feeling to animals or to the utterly inanimate, as in, "the trees were sighing, the heavens were weeping." In the vocabulary of poetic criticism, this sort of rhetorical figure is called "pathetic fallacy," the fallacy of attributing *pathos* to the insentient, as in the story of the cruel vizier who promised his courtier a reward if he could guess correctly which of the vizier's eyes was the glass one. "The left," replied the courtier without hesitation. "How did you guess?" "It was the one that had pity in it."

To *anér/andrós*, then, were attached the Greek notions of maleness as opposed to plain humanity: *Andreía* was manly courage; an *androsphinx* was the kind with the body of a lion and a masculine head, such as the bearded sphinxes of Egypt that Greek travelers reported in awe – the native Greek sphinxes were female. And in modern scientific terminology, *andro-* in compounds indicates male sexuality or maleness: *androphorous* flowers bear male parts; *andromania* is a grown-up version of "boy-craziness," an exaggerated venereal interest in members of the male sex. Anything *androgynous* characteristically exhibits both male and female traits.

Gynophores, gynecomania, and *gynandrous* plants may be summoned up to represent the other side of the masculine-feminine lexicographic story. Greek *gyné/ gynaikós* meant "woman" (as opposed to man and, presumably, beast, though most classical dictionaries don't trouble to tell us so in so many words) and is cognate with English *queen* and its doublet *quean,* a word that dialectally means simply "woman," and which, archaically but more generally, means "an impudent woman." *Queen* and *quean,* if we may digress into the vaults of English vocabulary for a moment, are a very telling pair of words expressing two popular if extreme views of Western womankind: woman as goddess and woman as shameless hussy.

Hussy, incidentally, seems to be a shortening of "housewife." "Housewife" is itself an interesting hybrid. The *house* part is the same as the *hus-* of *husband,* literally, "a person who lives in a house." The *wife* part comes from the standard Old English word for "woman," as still seen in the word *fishwife,* "a woman who sells fish," *not* "someone with a fish for a spouse," and the expression *old wives' tale,* "a tale told by an old woman (of whatever marital status)." The word *woman* itself comes from Old English *wíf,* whence "wife," and *man* – whence "man," though the original meaning of Old English *man* was "person," or, more specifically, "adult person." The original Old English term for "man" was *wer,* which survives in modern English in the word *werewolf.*

It is hard to know exactly what to make of the "man"/ "woman" words in a language – especially English, which has borrowed so freely from so many other languages and cultures – for words often conceal just as much as they reveal. What can be inferred about the relative status of man and woman, and their day-to-day dealings, from the vocabulary that is a culture's common currency? What can we guess about the Greeks from the words that have come down to us expressing their own sociosexual relationships?

The story is a complicated one, for Greece was never really a single society, just as Greek was never really a single language. Further, in any given section of Greece, whether Athens, Sparta, Thrace, Lesbos, or Kos, the relative status of women and men was a sometime, someplace thing. In conservative Athens, women were generally considered fertile fields in which the male seed might be sown to produce children, preferably male, so Athenian women were mostly confined to quarters, living out their dreary lives in badly lit, badly ventilated rooms, and ill-fed into the bargain. In Athens, the girls were fed less than the boys on the theory that males were needed for the army and there wasn't enough food to go around in nonagrarian Athens to feed *everybody*.

Athenian men customarily served ten years in the army, and it was generally assumed that there ought to be a ten-year difference in ages between spouses, older men marrying younger women. This was partly a matter of primitive birth control in a land where the mechanics of reproduction were not very well understood and a population boom (especially if it involved a normal number of noncombatant female births) could spell disaster for the local economy. (Extra males could be sent to war to be killed off or to return with their shields full of foreign lucre.) The other part of it seems to have been that the Athenian male aristocracy felt an ongoing need for local victims, and women were graciously allowed to swell the ranks of slaves and children when the need for social one-upmanship reared its bearded head.

Other Greek city-states were not nearly so blatantly sexist in their everyday dealings. In Sparta, women were treated with much greater respect than they were in Athens: As children they were fed as well as males and were sent to school to learn the same things as boys – *mens sana in corpore sano*. As a rule, women in Sparta had many more substantial legal rights than Athenian women did when it came to ownership of personal property and inheritance of familial goodies. And while Spartan marriage customs were not much better for women than the Athenian ones, what with the lengthy term of military service imposed on the Spartan males, at least (a) Spartan males were allowed to marry younger and (b) Spartan females were allowed extramarital liaisons with members of the same sex in a way that Athenians were not.

Athenian males were allowed to form homosexual liaisons, in fact, were encouraged to do so to some extent: The affectionate relationship between tutor and tutee, for example, is praised in such works as Plato's Socratic dialogue *Lysis;* and hoplites frequently operated on a buddy system in which another soldier in the square was not only friend but lover, a relationship that was applauded since the two soldiers would then be expected to look out for each other, especially in battle. The gods themselves were said to enjoy both heterosexual and homosexual affairs: Ganymede, Zeus's cup-bearer, started out as his beloved.

Female homosexuality, on the other hand, is not well-documented in Athenian literature, though this doesn't mean it didn't exist. That Athenian women were mostly kept illiterate and were largely excluded from the intellectual life of the city would have precluded serious documentation of their lives. But Sarah Pomeroy, in her highly readable and enlightening *Goddesses, Whores, Wives, and Slaves,* offers the hypothesis that female homosexuality tends to be best attested in places like Sparta and Lesbos, where women were generally held in high regard, places in which *any* reasonable person would wish to have a woman as a friend and lover.

The island of Lesbos (whence our word "lesbian") was the home of one of the greatest poets of antiquity, Sappho, who lived from roughly 650 B.C. into the next century. Her eloquent and forthright lyrics stand in sharp contrast to the Athenian silence about the relationship of woman to woman. Consider, for example, her lament for Atthis, who had left her to study with a rival poet, Andromeda:

Those wonderful days that the two of us shared:
When the two of us were together, how you'd decorate
Your flowing locks with violets and baby rose buds,
Circling your sapling throat with countless floral necklaces;

And how fragrant was your youthful flesh
When the two of us were together on the daïs,
Soft, to which the delicate young women
Would carry all that an Ionian might desire . . .

Sappho seems to have been married and to have had a daughter, Kleïs, the subject of some of her sweetest songs. She also seems to have had a brother in the wine trade whom she rebukes in one of her poems for squandering a great deal of money buying an Egyptian slave-courtesan's freedom and then setting her up in business.

Men of means did, from time to time, buy the freedom and the favors of slave women and courtesans, and were generally ridiculed for it by their fellow men – and their free-born wives. The courtesans were presumably somewhat more sanguine, since their profession was one of the very few open to unmarried women in ancient Greece allowing not only a measure of financial freedom but access to the intellectual life of the times as well.

DELTA

IS FOR *DIAGNOSIS* AND A MYRIAD OF other terms in the language of medicine that we have inherited from the Greeks – generally, if somewhat unfairly, credited with being the first Westerners to approach the related problems of the identification and treatment of disease in a systematic, scientific way. After all, according to the Greeks themselves, the Egyptians had already made great strides in the classification of humankind's various physical ills; and the ancient Persians, like many ancient peoples, believed that the chief cause of human ills was *diabolepsy* ("possession by an unkind spirit") and had what was arguably a reasonable way of treating disease: Call in the local priests and have them utter incantations and prayers for the recovery of the patient. And why not? If disease *was* caused by angry spirits, prayer was the obvious course of cure. Besides, as Dr. Benjamin Lee Gordon points out in his fascinating work, *Medicine throughout Antiquity*, there was something to be said for the fact that the Persians "resorted more frequently to spells than to drugs on the grounds that, although spells might not cure the disease, they at least would not kill the patient." In addition, Herodotus tells us that the Persian sick who wanted to hedge their bets would have their bedsteads set up in a public place and would ask passersby had *they* ever had a similar disease and, if so, what had they done to be cured of it – a far from irrational approach, really.

The tradition of Greek medicine begins with Aesculapius, the legendary semidivine offspring of the god Apollo and the utterly mortal Princess Koronis. Koronis later suffered the ill fortune of being shot down (literally) by Apollo's sister, Artemis, the virgin huntress, for having cuckolded her (Artemis's) brother who, in an unusual display of paternal feeling, snatched the yet unborn Aesculapius from the funeral fires. Aesculapius was then placed under the tutelage of the centaur Chiron who raised the lad, instructing him in the arts of healing. Unfortunately, Chiron did his work too well, teaching Aesculapius not only how to cure the sick but how to bring the very dead back to life. Zeus, sensing disastrous consequences for the divine order that propagation of this knowledge would entail, promptly and definitively took away Aesculapius's license to practice by blowing him away with a thunderbolt.

Nevertheless, the cult of Aesculapius grew rapidly, moving from the local temples where the healing process was essentially ritual, toward a more ambulatory priesthood possessing considerable practical experience in caring for the sick. By the sixth century B.C., hundreds of shrines all over the Greek-speaking world were functioning as prototypical hospitals. The Aesculapiades, as these physician-priests were called, came to include not merely the clergy but lay practitioners as well, though – shades of Zeus – the practice of Aesculapian medicine remained centered around the temples, for example, those at Kos and Knidos.

An essential feature of Aesculapian treatment was the "incubation sleep." The sick person would come to be examined by a process that the French centuries later termed *triage* ("a sorting out and classification of the wounded"). If not found to be a hopeless case, the patient was bathed, purged, made to abstain from wine and various foods, and bedded down for the night in the temple where, if all went well, he or she would receive oracular messages from the gods. The priests would then interpret these messages, often helping the patient along with a few judiciously chosen drugs, such as extract of poppy seed or sublethal – one hoped – dosages of hemlock.

This method had a rational madness to it: The Greek

way of dealing with disease up to this time had largely been to go for a good *prognosis* and let it go at that. (*Diagnosis* comes from the verb *diagignônai*, "to discern, render judgment," while *prognosis* comes from the verb *progignônai*, "to presage, to know in advance.") A *prognosis* told you what the outcome of the patient's malady was likely to be, while the *diagnosis* gave you some basis for treating the symptoms. The pre-Aesculapian means of ascertaining the prognosis was to have a *mántis* ("seer, diviner") come in and render an opinion as best he could, while in a state of divine ecstasy. His more sober understudy, the *prophḗtēs* ("prophet"), would put this into plain Greek. The physician could then take it away to the best of *his* abilities. The Aesculapiades were merely trying to eliminate a middleman or two by inducing the visions of the *mántis* in the patient and interpreting the patient's visions in-house.

Pythagoras (580–510 B.C.) and his followers, preoccupied as they were with number, order, and symmetry, ascribed three functions to human beings, each conveniently associated with specific parts of the body: One's "vegetable" functions were associated with the navel; "animal" functions with the heart; and "human" ones with the brain. The Pythagorean philosopher Empedocles (*ca.* 490–430 B.C.), a Sicilian, took this biomedical view of humankind a step farther, correlating the elements of fire, earth, water, and aether (air) with the bodily fluids of blood, phlegm, black bile, and yellow bile, respectively. This taxonomy of the *humors* (from Latin *humor*, "fluid") was to color medical thinking for the next two millennia, often with disastrous results when it came to the actual treatment of disease, as with the practice of blood-letting to remedy *dyscrasia* ("an imbalance of the humors"), a *delta* word better left forgotten.

Empedocles has another claim to fame: He postulated "preponderance of the male or female semen" at conception in the determination of sex of children, a notion

recent medical research has given some weight. Empedocles's postulate holds water to the extent that two distinct types of *zygote* have been identified under the
microscope, the androsperm and the gynosperm, which
seem to travel at different velocities and are apparently
sensitive to different intrauterine "climatic" conditions
involving the balance of alkaline to acid components.

It may also be said for Empedocles that, during an
epidemic, he advised the inhabitants of Selinus to clean
up the local water supply by diverting two nearby
streams, thus flushing out a fetid, stagnant pool that
surrounded the city. When this was done, the plague
abated. Although Empedocles, like most other learned
physicians of his time, attributed general pestilence to
the presence of unhealthy vapors, or *miasmas*, it is more
than likely that the real culprit was malaria, since ma-
larial mosquitoes love to breed in sewage swamps before
going off to infect the higher orders of creation. Empedocles was also credited with forestalling an epidemic
at his native Agrigentum by stopping up a chasm in a
neighboring hill through which a miasma was leaking, a
tall tale at best.

Democedes (who "flourished," as they say, toward
the end of the sixth century B.C.) is the first physician
of whom we have more than semimythical accounts.
Herodotus says that Democedes was hired by Darius
Nothos to treat a dislocated ankle sustained by the great
king in a fall from a horse. Democedes later turned up
as chief physician at Aegina (at a *talent* a year), then
was hired away to Athens at a hundred *minae* a year
(though Athenian money was a slightly lighter currency,
so the raise may not have been quite as great as 66%).
He was then hired away again, this time to serve under
Polycrates of Samos at *two* talents a year. Samos, however, fell to the Persians and Democedes once again
found himself working for Darius, again distinguishing
himself by successfully treating Atossa, Darius's queen,

for an abscess on her breast. Darius then allowed Democedes to return to Greece with the stipulation that he act
as guide to two Persian spies sent on reconnaissance for
what was to be the first of the Persian Wars. Once he
reached his native Krotona, however, Democedes balked
and the spies had to proceed without him.

By this time two rival schools of medicine had grown
up, associated with the Aesculapian temples at Kos and
Knidos. (Democedes seems to have been a Koan.) The
Knidians were largely diagnosticians and mystics, and
many of them visited the Persian court where they encountered Eastern theological healing. Ktesias, physician
to Artaxerxes Mnemon – he treated the spear wound that
the king sustained in hand-to-hand combat with Cyrus
at Kunaxa – was a Knidian. Thanks to his notes, we know
about several other Greek doctors in Persia, including the
hapless Appolonius of Kos, who was tortured for two
months and then buried alive as punishment for prac-
ticing "immoral medicine" on the Princess Amytis.
(Among the other tidbits of court gossip in his *Persica*,
Ktesias relates the story of the ingenious poisoning of
the noblewoman Statira by her rival, the Queen Mother
Parysatis. This ruthless woman cut a cooked bird in half
with a knife smeared with poison on one side, then ate
the other half "to show there was no deception." Statira
ate the tainted half and promptly expired.) Another
Knidian, Euryphon, practiced cautery – by some accounts,
to excess – and stated that the arteries contained blood,
and that certain diseases could arise from "insufficient
evacuation from the digestive tract."

The motto of the Knidian school was "accurate diagnosis; vigorous treatment." However, since the diagnosis
often was *not* accurate and the treatment more vigorous
than rational, the Knidians' patients did not always fare
much better than those in the hands of thaumaturgical
healers. At least one remedy used by the Knidians was
hellebore, of which Ktesias wrote:

Neither my father nor my grandfather before him ever dared to prescribe hellebore, since they simply hadn't the faintest idea of how to do it or what dosage to suggest. In those days, when somebody *did* prescribe hellebore, he customarily advised the patient to make out his last will and testament before taking the cure. . . .

The school of Kos was far more concerned with prognosis than with diagnosis: Given that a patient had a certain set of symptoms (what we now call a *syndrome*), what was likely to be the outcome of the disease? Hippocrates, born at Kos in 460 B.C. and unquestionably the foremost of the Koan physicians, put it this way:

Please don't quibble if the name of some specific disease which you have encountered isn't mentioned here, for you should be well able to recognize them all from the symptoms here delineated.

For his own part, Hippocrates was meticulous in recording the progress of diseases and the nature of symptoms; he left forty-two clinical histories and was not abashed to include twenty-five cases in which the patient died. Hippocrates was an Aesculapiade and drew freely on the traditional methods they used, saying that his predecessors had stumbled on much that was useful "in spite of so great a lack of knowledge." He firmly believed that the natural tendency of the body was to fight off disease, and thus viewed the proper physician as helping nature take its course rather than battling the malady with extraordinary or "heroic" remedies, or resorting to appeals for divine intervention. (In the Hippocratic Oath, surgery is left to the surgeons: *Surgery* comes from the Greek word for "hand," *cheír*, and was considered more of a trade than an art or science.) Accordingly, Hippocrates repeatedly stressed the importance of what we would today term the doctor's bedside manner, that is, the physician's capacity to work toward the patient's –

and the patient's family's – psychological well-being in a crisis. As Hippocrates himself put it:

The physician must not only know how – and when – to remain silent, but must lead a generally well-ordered life, for this will greatly enhance his reputation. . . . Boldness and impetuosity, though they may at times have their effect, are rarely well-received. . . . The physician must wear an expression of sympathy and understanding, never showing the slightest perplexity. . . . The physician must also bring to his labors the love of work and tenacity. . . .

Hippocrates justified the Koan emphasis on prognosis by arguing that the physician

will be all the more readily believed if he is able to predict the course of the disease in the presence of the sick, and people will all the more readily entrust themselves to his care with complete confidence. He who has foreseen what the course of the disease will be, will be in the best position to effect a cure . . . and, by predicting – and making explicit – who will live and who will die, the physician will insure himself against censure.

Perhaps the crowning glory of the school of Kos is the oath attributed to Hippocrates, still repeated in whole or in part by physicians in most Western countries at their swearing-in. The explicit prohibitions the oath contains against abortion and euthanasia – proof, it is said, that both of these practices were well known in ancient times – have carried much emotional weight when cited by modern foes of such practices. It is only fair to add that the oath also prohibits the physician from operating on a patient suffering from gallstones.

In other clauses, the oath-taker promises to

refrain from any willful act of mischief or corruption, and, further, from the seduction of females or males, freedmen or slaves. Whatever I shall see or hear, . . . I will not divulge to others, since all such information should be confidential.

It is quite possible that this last promise, subsequently guaranteed by law, began in the medical profession and was extended by analogy to confidences spoken to one's lawyer, priest, or spouse.

The medieval world owed much of its knowledge of Greek medicine to the Greco-Roman philosopher-physician Galen (Claudius Galenus) and the Arabian philosopher-physician Avicenna (Abū 'Alī al-Ḥusain ibn 'Abd'Allāh ibn Sīnā). Galen studied medicine in his native Mysia and, later, in Smyrna, Corinth, and Alexandria. Like many aspiring provincials of the time, Galen finally settled in Rome around 170 A.D. and served under the emperors Marcus Aurelius, Commodus, Sextus, and Severus. He wrote no fewer than fifteen commentaries on Hippocrates's works and, for his own part, engaged in pioneering work on the dissection of animals – human cadavers were still taboo – and is credited with being the first physician to diagnose by using the pulse.

Avicenna was born in southern Russia (Bokhara) in 980 A.D. and spent a good deal of his career in Persia, where he died in 1037. Basically a codifier whose philosophy leaned heavily on Aristotle and the Neo-Platonists, Avicenna served a variety of Near Eastern sultans, eventually being made vizier of Hamadan in Persia. A highly literate man, he was undoubtedly acquainted with the *Shahnamah,* a lengthy epic poem by the great Persian poet Abul Kasim Mansur Firdausi, which gives a history of the rulers of Persia, both legendary and authentic, and in which the semilegendary Emperor Jamshīd features prominently. Jamshīd was believed to have taught the Persians "leech-craft and the healing of the ill,/ The way to health, and the causes of disease." (Jamshīd was also said to have a cup that when he stared into it, would reveal the future.) Firdausi also recounts the visit of

Alexander the Great to an Indian Rājā – the northern Indian city of Sikandarābād takes its name from Alexander – who reputedly presented the great Greek king with several valuable slaves, including a beautiful woman, a wise philosopher, and a doctor skilled in diagnosis by the examination of the urine of the sick. It might be added that at least among the Muslims of Northern India in the nineteenth century, "Greek medicine" was preferred by many to the Ayurvedic (Hindu) tradition and to the new "English" medicine as well.

A final note on the letter *delta*: The letter's triangular upper-case form has given rise to a variety of "delta" words in English – "delta-wing" jets, "deltoid" muscles, and Mississippi "Delta" blues. The triangle symbol also shows up in the sign language of American hoboes with the following diagnostic/prognostic sense: One large triangle plus two or three littler ones chalked on the side of a house known for its charity advises the visiting hobo to "tell pitiful story."

EPSILON

IS FOR *EUREKA!* "*EUREKA!*" ("I'VE DIS-
covered [it]!") shouted Archimedes as, dripping, he
rushed forth from his bathtub and streaked down the
street. At least, this is the story school children have been
told for centuries, presumably as a lesson not to grow up
to be absentminded scientific types (think how silly
Archimedes must have looked to the good people of
Syracuse as he tore through the town, as naked as a
jaybird).

The whole hue and cry seems to have been over the
solution to a particularly knotty problem of practical
science that had come up in a case of suspected fraud.
Archimedes had been called in as a consultant by his
kinsman, Hieron, the king of Syracuse. The king had
commissioned a crown of gold and suspected the gold-
smith who did the job of having short-weighted him by
overalloying the goods with silver. The problem was that
while the *weight* of the crown could be verified easily
enough, its *density* could not. (Gold is substantially
denser – heavier by volume – than silver, but an ounce of
gold obviously weighs the same as an ounce of silver.)
And naturally nobody wanted to melt the crown down
to see how much silver was in it.

There are two versions of what happened in Archimedes's bath. In the first, Archimedes took off his clothes
and slowly immersed himself in the bathtub, which had
been filled completely with water. As the water cascaded
over the edge, Archimedes suddenly realized that the
volume of water that overflows a full container when
something is put into it is equal to the volume of that
something, such as a person, a crown, or an ingot of
silver. From there, it was a short step to comparing the

volume of water displaced by the crown and its equal weight in silver and gold.

The second version of the story is slightly more elegant (and does Archimedes's powers of observation far better justice). In this case, Archimedes took off his clothes and slowly immersed himself in the bathtub, which had *not* been filled all the way to the top, but rather to a more reasonable level. What Archimedes noticed, as he settled into buoyancy, was that the water level rose as his sensation of weight decreased. From this he concluded that there was a direct relationship between the weight an object lost in water, and the weight of the water it displaced (the difference between the Before and After waterlines around the inside of the tub), and furthermore that this relationship was one to one. Archimedes subsequently published the fruits of his researches on weights and water in his *Treatise on Floating Bodies*.

It is quite possible of course that the whole bathtub tale is utterly apocryphal. What *is* known about Archimedes – or has at least been supposed for centuries – is that he was first and foremost a geometer (which in those days meant a surveyor or, more generally, a practical mathematician). He appears to have been primarily interested in engineering and numerological problems for the challenges they posed to mathematical thinking. One of his more inspired treatises, *The Sand Reckoner* – dedicated to Hieron's son and successor, Gelon – posed the seemingly innocent question, "How many grains of sand are there in the universe?," which the author goes on to consider. In so doing, he offered a rigorous defense of the Greek alphabetic system of numeration, which he showed to be perfectly adequate (with a few minor adjustments) to the task of expressing quite large numbers, really.

Another of his treatises, while ostensibly concerned with determining how many head of cattle you have in your herd if it contains four different kinds of cattle of both sexes (whence the title of the work, *The Cattle Problem*), actually proves to be an elaborate exercise in solving simultaneous equations. This work, incidentally, is dedicated to Eratosthenes, whom Archimedes is said to have met on sabbatical in Alexandria. (Though sometimes known as "Beta" – i.e., "second-stringer" – among his rivals, Eratosthenes was generally held in very high esteem in his day. He spent the better part of his life in Alexandria on the payroll of Ptolemy III, the Greek king of Egypt, attacking such diverse problems as the measurement of the earth and the generation of prime numbers.) On this sabbatical in Egypt, Archimedes is reputed to have invented the boat-bailing sluice known as the Archimedean screw.

Plutarch says that Archimedes was disdainful of mere mechanical tasks; nevertheless, he served both Hieron and Gelon well, designing and supervising construction of sophisticated weaponry for the Syracusans' arsenal. In fact, one of his last projects was a battery of short-range catapults for the defense of the city against the besieging Romans. Syracuse, the major city in Sicily (and indeed of the whole of Magna Graecia) was a staging ground for both the Romans to the north and the Carthaginians to the south in their chronic squabbling. The Syracusans were usually up in arms, either to take sides or to defend their neutrality. When the Romans finally took the city in 212 B.C., Archimedes was among the civilian casualties. It is said that a Roman soldier came upon Archimedes as he was drawing diagrams of a thorny geometrical problem in the dirt. The soldier asked him what he was doing, and Archimedes is reputed to have told the soldier to go away and stop blocking his light, at which point the soldier struck him dead. (The moral being: If you insist on being an absentminded scientific type, all well and good, but you'd better watch your mouth.)

Archimedes was around seventy-five years old when he met his end, Eratosthenes's elder by some fifteen years. His tombstone (which Cicero claimed to have restored

two hundred years later while he was quaestor of Sicily)
bore the image of a sphere inscribed in a cylinder, com-
memorating Archimedes's demonstration of the ratios of
their surface areas and volumes.

Now it should perhaps be said in the interest of scientific rigor that what Archimedes *really* cried as he rushed
dripping from the bath was not *"Eureka!"* at all, but
rather *"Heúrēka!"* The Greeks were curiously casual
about representing their *h* sound in writing, sometimes
not bothering to write it at all. As a result, the Romans
often borrowed Greek words as though they had no
initial *h* in them. In any event, if Archimedes said it at
all, it would undoubtedly have been *"Heúrēka!"* and not
"Eureka!" – unless, of course, he was whispering.

The same verb – *heureîn*, "to discover, find" – also gives
us the word *heuristic*, which basically means "inventive"
but has gradually taken on the connotation of "self-
instructive." A heuristic computer program, for example,
is a set of instructions that involves automatically altering itself on the basis of the data processed. Thus, the
computer modifies its behavior by examining its past
experience and discarding things that didn't work out.
Probably the most famous heuristic programs have been
chess-playing ones. One of the authors played a "naïve"
program – it had been in operation for a very short time –
and was ignominiously forced to resign on the twenty-
first move. Such an opponent is, of course, impervious
to bluff.

Another form of heuristic program is now commonly
in use as an aid to doctors in the diagnosis of the variety
of human ills. The computer churns through a mountain
of statistical information in short order and gives its best
guess as to what's ailing you; then you go into the computer as part of the statistical file, altering it slightly. It
would naturally be possible to skew the statistics – and the
diagnoses based upon them – by bringing along a group of
friends who share a rare tropical disease when you go in
to have your sniffle read; but so far, nobody seems to
have bothered.

‹ Z ›

ZETA

IS FOR *ZEUS* – AND FOR ZOO. THE FIRST
systematic documentation of the life and times of the
Greek pantheon that has survived to posterity is Hesiod's
Theogony (*The Origin of the Gods*), which seems to
have hit the stands at some point during the eighth
century B.C. and has remained on the classical best-seller
list ever since. The work is an apparent fusion of many
local traditions treating – as the poet succinctly puts it –
"the same gods under different names." This seems to
have troubled no one at the time, there being a general
readiness, indeed, almost eagerness, to see parallels between local gods and those of one's neighbors (perhaps
as a means of increasing a sense of community with the
world at large in an era of general isolation).

Thus, Herodotus, in describing the customs of the
Egyptians, is quick to call Osiris "the Egyptian Adonis"
because of the similarities between the death and resur-
rection stories about the two. Some centuries later,
George Frazer, in his monumental *Golden Bough*, was
equally quick to classify *all* god-that-dies-and-is-resur-
rected myths under the same heading, suggesting an
essentially common origin. Whether they perceived it as
literally, historically true, the Greeks would, one supposes, have been happy enough to believe it. The notion
made life tidy and, if nothing else, would have given the
Athenians and the Thracians, the Spartans and the Les-
bians, something in common to talk about on those rare
occasions when gathered in the same room, perhaps
along with a random Babylonian, renegade Persian, or
itinerant Egyptian.

What follows, then, is a consensual summary of the
articles of faith to which most Greeks would have sub-
scribed, allowing ample room for local variation.

In the beginning was Chaos, which, then as now, meant Disorder, though it was also perceived as an entity with sufficient internal organization to be able to give birth to Gaia (Mother Earth) and Ouranos (Father Sky). (Some held that Gaia was the only offspring of Chaos and that it was she who produced Ouranos.) Gaia promptly mated with Ouranos to produce the Titans; the three Cyclopes (or one-eyed ones), of whose children the most famous was Polyphemus, blinded by the crafty Odysseus; and the three Hekatoncheires (or hundred-handed ones). Then, fatigued by all of this child-bearing – the Titans were, after all, giants – Gaia conspired with her children to castrate Ouranos. The one to bell the cat, as it fell out, was Kronos, the youngest of the lot, who took the cosmic sickle fashioned by his mother and did the dreadful deed. As his reward he got the right to rule the universe with his sister-consort Rhea, thereby setting a precedent for all manner of folk tales that have the youngest kids take responsibility and reap the rewards in the end, whether they get to marry their siblings or not.

Kronos, who was no fool, did not wish to be unseated or unmanned by any of his own offspring and so made it a policy to swallow up each of them as soon as they were born. After a number of births and swallowings, however, Rhea managed to spirit away their last offspring, Zeus, substituting a stone wrapped in swaddling clothes, all of which suggests that Kronos was either terribly myopic or woefully inexperienced in the art of parenting, or both.

Zeus's first consort was Metis, the daughter of the Titan Okeanos, god of the outer ocean. Metis managed to cause Kronos to regurgitate all of Zeus's siblings – the Olympians Hades, Poseidon, Hera, Demeter, and Hestia – who, with Zeus, raised an insurrection against their father. Kronos aligned himself with the unswallowed Titans, save for Prometheus (who with the gift of foresight, knew on which side of the bread the butter was to be found) and Epimetheus (who, with the gift of hindsight, for what it was worth in those days, seems to have come along mainly for the ride). The Olympians also had on their side the Hekatoncheires, who set up shop manufacturing thunderbolts, thus becoming the world's first munitions workers.

In the fireworks that followed, the Olympians dug in up in heaven and the Titans attempted to raise a siege-tower by piling Mounts Pelion and Ossa on top of Mount Olympus, an act still proverbial for grandiose if futile tour de force. When the dust had cleared, the Olympians had won the battle, and the defeated Titans – with the exceptions of Prometheus, Epimetheus, and Atlas (given the task of holding up the sky forever, with a time-out to go fetch the golden apples of the Hesperides for Herakles) – were sent to spend the rest of their days in Tartarus, the part of the Greek underworld corresponding to our hell. And as for Prometheus and Epimetheus, they didn't make out all that well either: Prometheus eventually came to grief by giving mankind fire from the Olympians' altar. Zeus, ever one for keeping the mortals in their place, chained him to a rock and sent a vulture every day to peck away at his liver – but that is another story. Epimetheus wound up married to Pandora, whose insatiable curiosity caused her to open a chest, loosing all of the world's evils and pains on humanity, which just goes to show how useful hindsight is.

The Olympians then set up shop atop Mount Olympus, whence their name. Zeus got jurisdiction over the universe, save for the watery places, which were given to Poseidon to rule, and the underworld, which was given to Hades. The watery places included the seas, rather generous, given the Greek knowledge of the world. The underworld wasn't insubstantial either: It included everything under the earth – mineral deposits and whatnot – and the tripartite region where dead people and demigods went after their time on earth was done. If you were judged to be a good guy, you went to the Elysian Fields to frolic and play. If you were judged to have been neither particularly good nor particularly bad, you were dispatched to the Asphodel Fields; if you were bad, you went to Tartarus, which was your tough luck. Good guys, furthermore, got to drink from the River of Memory if they liked; otherwise, they were obliged to drink from the river of forgetfulness, Lethe (whence our words "lethargic" and "lethal").

The other Olympians did not go unrewarded. Hestia was made patroness of hearth and home, remaining a virgin for the rest of her days (and nights); Demeter was put in charge of harvests and was greatly loved and respected by humankind; and Hera got to marry Zeus. Metis was conveniently gotten out of the way by the simple expedient of Zeus's swallowing her. She was pregnant at the time with Athena, who was subsequently born from Zeus's forehead with assistance from a hammer blow by Hephaestos, the Greek Vulcan, patron of blacksmiths and volcanoes. Clearly, Zeus's sisters did not make out as well as the boys in the Olympian family, though in comparison to mortals of the day, they didn't do too badly.

Zeus gets his name, etymologically, from a Proto-Indo-European noun that seems to have meant something like "luminous sky, daytime sky." The word shows up in Sanskrit as *dyāus*, "day, luminous heaven" and *dyāuhpitā*, "sky-father," cognate with Latin *Jupiter*. Other cognates include Latin *diēs*, "*day*"; *deus*, "god"; and *Diana* (Artemis in Greek), sister to Apollo; to which may be added Germanic *Tiu* (whence our word "Tuesday") and Norse *Tyr*, both sky/war gods like Zeus.

The Greek association of Zeus with the heavens fits in well enough with their basically tripartite view of the cosmos: Sky/heaven was plainly above; the earth was here; and the underground was underneath. Whether the surrounding ocean – *ōkeanós* – counted as a fourth part seems to have been a matter of some debate. In any event, this division of reality into a giant layer cake had a certain appeal, though by the fifth century B.C., many scientifically-minded Greeks had begun to suspect that things were not quite so neat and simple. For example, the earth might really be a sphere instead of a layer cake: As early as the third century B.C., Eratosthenes went so far as to calculate the circumference of the spherical earth by measuring the disparity at noon between shadows cast by poles of similar height at two places of known distance from each other; this calculation by no means put the pantheon out of business.

We might add in passing that the Indo-European inhabitants of India had a similarly tripartite view of the cosmos, though with a slight difference: There was earth, and there was heaven, but there was also a space in between the two – the Ether or *Antariksha*, literally, "the place between the two dwelling places." These were created by the Lord Vishnu in three mighty steps: First, the earth was created (with room in the cellar for the dead); second, the *Antariksha* (no-man's-land); and third, heaven, the abode of the gods. As in the Greek system, the Indian gods were free to pop down to earth to meddle in the lives of the local human denizens when they had no better way to amuse themselves.

But back to Zeus, a fellow whose character was not, perhaps, all that one might wish to see in the mightiest of philosopher-kings. The fact that he usurped the throne of the universe was not particularly troublesome to the Greeks, who were used to this sort of thing. A *týrannos*, "usurper," wasn't necessarily evil, as the word "tyrant" has come to suggest, any more than a *basileús*, "hereditary successor to the throne," was necessarily good. (Indeed, the chilling pivotal point in Sophocles's *Oedipus Rex* comes when an ambassador salutes Oedipus, who up to this time has been called *týrannos*, as *basileús* – true king, but of Corinth, not Thebes – and thus sets into motion the unraveling of the true and terrible story of Oedipus's parentage.) Nor did the Greeks seem to find Zeus's castrating his father, gobbling up his children, or marrying his sister at all unsettling.

What *did* bother at least some Greeks was Zeus's

obvious propensity for extramarital dalliance, mostly with mortal members of the opposite sex. Mating with local tutelary goddesses was one thing (it has been argued that these liaisons served to put an official kibosh on the local matriarchy by institutionalizing patriarchal invasion and forceful take-over). But seducing virtually any unprotected woman, usually by subterfuge, was not behavior one might expect of the lord of lords, no matter what one's sexual or social orientation.

And indeed Zeus's conquests were as numerous as they were notorious. He managed to seduce Danaë – who had been sequestered in a tower, like Rapunzel, against just such an eventuality – by visiting her in the form of a shower of gold. (Freudians may make of this whatever they please.) Leda he deflowered by sneaking up in the guise of a swan; and he ran Europa down in the form of a bull. That Danaë produced Perseus, the slayer of the Gorgon Medusa, and Leda produced Castor and Pollux, the twin gods of the Spartans, may or may not have been of some consolation to them, though one wonders in any case why Zeus felt called upon to be so sneaky. In a slight variation on this tactic of animal peekaboo, Zeus turned one of his objects of affection, Io, into a calf. The long-suffering and feisty Hera wasn't fooled for a moment: She dispatched a gadfly to chase the poor creature out of Greece, over the Bosporus (literally, "cow-crossing"), and all the way to Egypt. There, recovering her human form, Io gave birth to Epaphus, later king in his adopted country and founder of the great city of Memphis.

This sort of randy gallivanting engendered not a little cynicism among educated Greeks, and the Romans after them, who judged that if the gods were indeed divine, they wouldn't go waltzing about like so many humans or beasts of the forest, pouncing on anything that moved. Nevertheless, the Athenians had an official attitude of reverence for the gods with all their warts: However capricious Zeus and the others might seem, blasphemy was a capital offense – and a frequent charge brought against troublesome philosophers like Socrates, much as income tax evasion is the modern means of bringing low gangland slayers, drug traffickers, and a host of politically problematic free-thinkers when no better ground for harassment presents itself. That the gods and their exploits smacked of human creation was of little note.

The more cautious philosophers preferred to take a middle ground, doubting out loud the more lurid Zeus legends, yet revering him for those attributes that *anyone* would be willing to call godly. Thus, Plutarch, in his dialogue entitled "The Decline of the Oracles," says,

Now the qualities which we must naturally attribute to all godly deeds are these: moderation, sufficiency, lack of excess, and utter self-responsibility,

quoting elsewhere a hymn to Zeus that he attributes to Orpheus (one of the few mortals who managed to go to hell and return, however briefly, to tell the tale):

Zeus the beginning, Zeus the middle – all things come from Zeus.

If the Greeks were eager for any new wrinkle on the Olympian pantheon, they were just as interested in any new wrinkle on the animal kingdom here on earth; and if they were happy to hear any new story about the gods of foreign lands, they were equally happy, if not more so, to hear about new and wonderful exotic earthly animals. The Greeks were not alone in this. Everybody in the ancient world was curious to know what sorts of living creatures shared the earth with them, and, for those who could afford it, at least *some* of the fabulous beasts reported by returning travelers could actually be seen face to face at the *zoo*.

The first zoos or *zoological gardens*, if we discount the legendary Noah's, were probably those belonging to the Egyptian nobility, though it is possible that the Chinese

Emperor Wen-wang's "Park of Intelligence" in Hunan antedated even these. In any case, the first recorded zoo in the Western world was that of the Egyptian Queen Hatasu, who ruled at the turn of the sixteenth century B.C. and who sent an expedition along the African east coast to collect, among other things, interesting indigenous animals, which she installed in her "Garden of Amen." Succeeding pharaohs continued the practice of adding exotic beasts to their collection, as did the Ptolemies after Alexander the Great's conquest of Egypt. Indeed, Alexander was so fascinated by the variety of animals he encountered in his extensive travels, he had his old tutor, Aristotle, oversee a number of animal-collecting expeditions, the results of which are recorded in Aristotle's *Historia Animalium*.

The word *zoo* comes ultimately from the Greek *zōón*, "living thing." Thus, *protozoa* are the *first* living things – amoebas, paramecia, and so on – that inhabit fresh water untouched by civilization and chlorine. Geological eras are named after the fauna living at those times: Paleozoic (from *palaiós*, "ancient," the one in which the most ancient forms of life appeared); Mesozoic (from *mésos*, "middle," in which the not-so-old and not-so-new forms of life appeared, including such notables as Brontosaurus, "thunder-lizard," and Tyrannosaurus Rex, "tyrant-lizard"); and Cenozoic (from *kainós*, "new," among whose more notable inhabitants are the many forms of humankind).

There is, alas, no plausible connection to be made between the letter *zeta* and the Mayan bat-god Zotz.

⊣ H ⊢

ETA

IS FOR *HELIOS*, THE DIVINE PERSONI-
fication of the sun, and for all of the *helio-* words in
English – *heliocentric, heliotrope, heliozoan, helium,* and
the like – derived from Greek *hélios,* "the sun." *Eta* is in
fact doubly for *Helios* and its offspring, since this letter
underlies the Greek orthographic signs for both *h* and *ē*.
The Phoenician alphabet, which the Greeks eagerly
adopted as their own, was fairly casual about representing
vowel sounds, a general characteristic of the Semitic
writing systems down to this very day. The only true-blue
vowel sign in the Phoenician alphabet was *aleph,* which
the Greeks took over as the sign for their *a* sound, *alpha.*

Phoenician *yod* and *waw,* representing the so-called
semivowels, *y* and *w* in that language, were taken over
by the Greeks to represent their own *y* and *i,* and *w* and
u, more or less respectively. "More or less" must be added
by way of honest qualification since, as it worked out,
while Phoenician *yod* – Greek *iota* – gave us *i* (and somewhat later, *j*), *waw* was a real can of worms: It not only
gave us our *u* and, later, *v,* and still later, *w* – double-*u* –
and, in its upper-case version, *y,* but our *f* as well. To
add to the general confusion, *yod* and *waw* also do at
least double duty in modern Yiddish and Ladino – Yiddish being a dialect of Medieval German and Ladino, a
dialect of Medieval Spanish, each spoken in the modern
world and each written in Hebrew script. In Yiddish, *yod*
represents both *y* and *i,* while *waw* (*vav*) represents both
v and *u.*

The Phoenician letter *'ayin* (originally the letter
chosen to represent the Phoenician consonantal glottal
stop) does similar double service, appearing as the letter
for *e* in Yiddish (and Ladino) and the short *o, omicron,*

in Greek. The Greeks went on to adopt a run-together version for their lower-case long o, *omega*.

The two remaining vowels in the Greek phonetic inventory, short and long *e*, wound up being represented by the Phoenician letters *he* (whence *epsilon*, plain *e*) and *ḥeth* (whence *eta*). Ḥeth was also used, in modified form, to represent the Greek *h* sound at the beginning of words: The upper-case form of the letter *H* was broken in half (⊢ ⊣) and, after some experimentation, all but the upper part of the left-hand half (⌐) was written above the initial vowel. Thus, for example, *hélios* would have been written with an initial *eta* surmounted by the right-facing remainder of the Phoenician letter *ḥeth*, acknowledging the phonetic character of the aspirated *h*, whatever the following vowel might be.

We may add as a footnote to all this that the Greeks, whether out of a sense of symmetry or fairness or because they couldn't bear to see it go to waste, took the left-facing remainder of the letter *ḥeth* and wrote it over all those initial vowels in words that didn't begin with *h*. Thus, for example, the name of the letter *epsilon* was written with this left-facing mark (⊣) over the initial *e*. The right-facing mark is known as the *spiritus asper*, "rough breathing," while the left-facing mark is known as the *spiritus lenis*, "smooth breathing."

But back to *hélios*, cognate, believe it or not, with Latin *sol*, "sun," their common ancestor having been something on the order of **sawel*, from which the *w* disappeared, allowing the two vowels to elide, and whose initial *s* became *h* in Greek. While *hélios*, the sun, was sometimes personified as Helios, the sun god, the Greeks generally preferred to associate the sun in its godly aspect with Apollo, who moonlighted, so to speak, as the patron of the Muses (and, by extension, the arts) and one of the gods of pestilence. It was Apollo in this latter capacity to whom the citizens of Thebes prayed for advice on how to cure the plague that gripped the city at the start of the events recorded in Sophocles's *Oedipus Rex*.

Apollo was popularly thought to drive his sun-chariot across the sky daily, much as Ra in Egypt sailed through the heavens in his solar boat. One myth relates that Phaeton, Apollo's son, having begged his father to let him drive the sun-chariot for a day, got his wish at last but lost control when the horses, sensing a strange hand on the reins, cut loose. The chariot was dragged close to the earth, scorching the deserts of Syria and Africa and burning the inhabitants black. Phaeton was thrown from the chariot and killed. (The parallels with the story of Daedalus and Icarus, another hoary moral tale about what happens to children who disobey their parents, are as plain as day.) In the late nineteenth century, a fashionable type of horse-drawn buggy was dubbed a phaeton, a most suitable conveyance for the daring young blades of the upper classes. The phaeton later gave way to its more high-powered automotive descendants, the Comet and the Mercury.

The Indo-Europeans have tended to see the sun as a male god and the moon goddess as a female, though there is no intrinsic reason why the gender associations should be sun-male, moon-female except, perhaps, for the correlation between the moon's phases and the female menstrual cycle. Indeed, other peoples of the world have reversed these roles: The Eskimos have a folk tale about the brother-sister relationship enjoyed by these two celestial orbs in which the sun is the sister and the moon is the cold and irresponsible brother.

But whatever its gender, the sun has been the focus of a great deal of attention, both devotional and scientific. The Hittites, for example, had a hymn to the sun that began: "O Great Sun God, You look into the heart of man, but no one can look into Your heart. If anyone does evil, the Sun God is there," a testament as much to the sun's physical properties as to its divine powers. Indeed, it is a short step from the sun's regularity and omnipresence, its considerable warming and nurturing capabilities, to its personification as the ultimate arbiter of cosmic justice, echoed perhaps in Jacques Prévert's modern-day poem, which begins, "Our Father Who art in heaven, stay there . . ."

The inscrutable Egyptian king Akhnaten put not too fine a point on it when he declared that there was no god the equal of Aten, the sun-disc. This "heresy" so shook up the local clergy that, after his death, they did not content themselves with merely reinstating the old polytheistic religion of the troubled state but had many of Akhnaten's monuments and inscriptions defaced or utterly destroyed, even though he *had* been married to the wise and strikingly beautiful Nefertiti. (Tutankhamen, Akhnaten's nephew, who succeeded to the throne when a mere child, was little more than a pawn in this mysterious antisolar upheaval – the Millard Fillmore of fourteenth century B.C.) Freud, in his *Moses and Monotheism*, claimed that Akhnaten's monotheism, such as it was, was the source for the monotheism of the Jews, though his argument leaves something to be desired from the standpoint of modern anthropology. But who knows?

Although the Athenian state religion sanctioned a host of anthropomorphic views of the sun, moon, and stars, Greek philosophers fairly early had noted the clocklike regularity of solar and lunar motion – more characteristic of a faithful servant than of a god. Thales of Miletus is even credited with having predicted a solar eclipse in the sixth century B.C., though the story may well be spurious. It is certainly so, however, that Anaxagoras, on the basis of his own observation and reasoning, taught in Athens a century later that the sun was a mass of fiery stone, which he reckoned to be roughly the size of the Peloponnese. For which the modern student should give him at least a passing grade, though the authorities of the time arrested him for blasphemy. He escaped death only through the graceful eloquence of Pericles, who managed to get the sentence reduced to perpetual exile.

Two hundred years later still, Aristarchus taught that day and night were the result of the earth's rotation and that the earth described an orbit around the sun, rather than vice versa, this in contrast to the fictitious twentieth-century scholar, de Selby, who taught that night was "an accretion of black air." Aristarchus also attempted to measure the relative sizes of the sun and the moon by the judicious application of the principles of geometry (literally, "measurement of the earth"), though his techniques failed him in the end: his figures of nineteen to one were thoroughly disbelieved by his contemporaries. Hipparchus, who lived in the second century B.C., did not accept Aristarchus's heliocentric model of the universe, though he did somehow manage to give an accurate description of the mechanics of both solar and lunar eclipses.

It is well to remember that these philosophers represented a very small minority of even the literate classes of Greek society. For the tradesman, sailor, farmer, and goatherd, the idea of a benevolent Apollo regularly driving his sun-chariot across the sky was not only adequate but the very essence of "God's in his heaven, all's right with the world." And if the modern reader feels a bit smug at this point, he or she has only to hearken to that peculiar gut feeling that everyone gets during an eclipse of the sun – the terrible sight of the old familiar sun eroded to a sliver of itself, the chill wind that rushes in from nowhere as totality approaches – or even to that milder malaise accompanying the shortened days and lengthened shadows at the approach of the winter solstice, the "baleful light" of the Latin poet Ausonius and the "evening all afternoon" of the American poet Wallace Stevens.

So what do we think we know about the sun in this present day and age? Well, we are alive to the fact that the sun is large, and hot, and old, and very far away, and without it, we would be in very bad shape indeed. Some still say that there is nothing new under the sun, while others maintain that the sun is the only hope for the future. All of this is undoubtedly so, though the dreadful knowledge of the sun's *modus operandi*, nuclear fusion – and its opposite number, nuclear fission – may well one day result in the extermination of all life on this particular planet, a possibility never dreamed of by the Greeks in all their sword-rattling fury.

But let us talk about the ever so much milder moon. One of the Greek words for this marvelous celestial presence was *selénē*. The Greek moon goddess was variously known as Selénē or Artemis, sister of Apollo, and, like him, a plague-broker – the English word *lunacy* comes from the Latin word for the moon. But, whatever else may be said against her, Selénē's temple at Ephesus was reckoned one of the seven wonders of the ancient world. (The other six were the Colossus of Rhodes, the tomb of Mausolos – the original mausoleum, the hanging gardens of Babylon, the statue of Zeus at Olympia, the lighthouse at Alexandria, and the pyramids of Egypt, of which only the last have survived to modern times.) At Ephesus, the scene of Saint Paul's less than warm reception when he came to preach the Word, the moon goddess was represented as a many-breasted mother figure. Elsewhere, Artemis, the virgin huntress with the silver bow, remained the protector of all suckling creatures though adamant in her refusal to dally with the opposite sex, or to allow any of her handmaidens to do so either. Her heritage is that of the Babylonian Ishtar and the Phoenician Astarte, both formidable figures with whom no right-thinking person would wish to tangle on any dark night.

The other Greek word for moon, *ménē*, is cognate with our own and is related to our "month" and "measure" (the latter from Latin via French), and "menstruation" and "trimester," the original idea having been, apparently, that the moon was a handy measuring device. (The Latin word for moon, *luna*, like Greek *selénē*, has its roots in a word meaning "light, brightness.") The seafaring Greeks well knew the effects of the moon on the tides, and were as familiar with its phases as they were with the apparently regular comings and goings of the sun, so it is hardly surprising that both the sun and the moon featured prominently in the reckoning of time.

By and large, the Greeks were content to measure time by the day, though smaller units of time could be calculated after a fashion through the use of the *heliotrope*, or sundial, and that ingenious device, the *clepsydra*, or "water-clock" (literally, "water-thief"). The clepsydra was simply a pair of bowls, one set atop the other. Water was allowed to pour at a regular rate from the upper bowl into the lower one. This time-keeping mechanism was used in the courts: You had however-many bowls of water to plead your case or make rebuttal, and if, for some reason, the proceedings were interrupted, the upper bowl was stoppered until it was time to resume the business at hand, at which point, the water was allowed to flow again.

Generally, though, days, months, seasons, and years were the temporal stock-in-trade of the Greeks, as they had been for nearly everybody else in the ancient world. True, the Romans had a word for "hour," *hora*, but as a unit for reckoning time it left something to be desired: Each Roman day (from sunrise to sunset) was divided into twelve *horae*, regardless of the actual length of the day, so the *hora* had no real fixed value. And pay, for Roman workers as for their Greek counterparts, was by the day, the notion of the hourly wage being a relatively modern invention.

The much-maligned Middle Ages brought, with other technical and scientific innovations, the first true mechanical clock to strike the hours as we now know them. Not everyone was happy about this triumph of human invention (proudly mounted on the church of Saint Gothard in Milan) or the regularity it brought to people's lives. While one contemporary is recorded as saying in admiration of the new Milanese clock that "it distinguishes one hour from another, which is of greatest use to men of every degree," workers of the world obliged to punch in and out ever since, have often grumbled that their employers never had a better opportunity to pick pockets, in spite of "time and a half," "double time," and "turn-around time." And workers are not alone in their sometime resentment of the rigid ticking away of the hours: While the Roman Catholic Church begrudgingly accepted this new means of reckoning time, the Eastern Orthodox Church would have none of it, arguing that "the mathematical division of time into hours, minutes, and seconds has no relationship with the eternity of time." Accordingly, up until the end of the last century, no Eastern Orthodox church would install a mechanical clock on or within its walls.

THETA

IS FOR *THEATER* AND *THESPIS*, NOT
to be confused with Thespios, all but one of whose fifty
daughters slept with the energetic Herakles during his
stay at Thespiae at the foot of Mount Helicon while
searching for the lion of Cithaeron. *Thespis* was the
semilegendary playwright and *metteur-en-scène* whom
Aristotle credited with revolutionizing Greek drama in
the latter part of the sixth century B.C. by the simple
expedient of introducing a solo actor to play Mr. Bones
to the chorus leader's Mr. Interlocutor. Prior to this
time, Greek drama had consisted of a chorus and its
leader metrically running down the exploits of the god
Dionysus at the annual spring festival in his honor, accompanied by much singing, dancing, and general vernal
fertility-riting. The appearance of a solo actor, called a
hypokrités, "answerer" (whence our word *hypocrite*,
i.e., "actor, dissembler"), set the stage, as it were, for a
variety of radical changes in the life of the Greek *theater*
in both its senses – theater as drama and theater as the
place in which drama is presented.

As far as theater in the sense of drama is concerned,
the introduction of one solo actor opened the way for
the addition of other solo actors to liven things up.
Aristotle credits Aeschylus, said to have been born some
ten years after Thespis's theatrical innovation, with the
addition of a second solo performer. (Aeschylus is also
said to have been the inventor of the padded buskin, that
is, elevator shoes, to give the players greater visibility on
stage.) Sophocles, Aeschylus's junior by some thirty
years, is said to have introduced a third and fourth solo
actor and the use of a painted backdrop to provide a little
scenery, the original function of the backdrop having

been simply to hide the troupers' dressing room from the spectators.

The physical layout of the theater (literally, "place for viewing") was changed from a circle in which the chorus and chorus leader performed around a central altar with the onlookers ringed around the periphery, to the now-familiar semicircle and stage arrangement so that the solo actors could address their remarks to the audience without having to turn around every which way in midsentence.

Was Thespis a real person? Aristotle and tradition say yes, but others, notably Lord Raglan in his seminal work, *The Hero*, say no. Aristotle's argument, to the extent that the point was argued at all, held that everybody believed the story of Thespis and *somebody* must have been responsible for the introduction of a solo actor into the theater, so why not he? Raglan counters by saying that believing doesn't make anything so, and how could a single person be responsible for such an important innovation with such far-reaching ritualistic implications anyway? Perhaps agnosticism here, to the extent that it makes any difference one way or the other, is the safest course, though confidentially, we're inclined to go with Raglan.

Whatever the case, Thespis is still very much with us, in part due to, of all people, Gilbert and Sullivan. In 1871, the ever irascible and irreverent W. S. Gilbert wrote the libretto *Thespis, or, The Gods Grown Old*, a masterful spoof in which a theater company – "used to take long parts on the shortest notice," as its producer-director Thespis reassures Zeus – offers to fill in for the Olympians while the latter go down to earth to see why their worship has fallen off so badly in recent years and what, if anything, they can do about it. The Thespians promptly bungle it: Mars is played by a sissy; Bacchus (Dionysus) is represented by the troupe's recently reformed drunk; the interim Athena is a virtual illiterate, and so on. When the gods return, they expel the actors, sentencing them to become "eminent tragedians/Whom no one ever, ever goes to see!"

Despite its music by the already popular Arthur Sullivan, this first collaboration between the two greats of the English stage was a dismal failure, folding after a month's run. Indeed, Sir Arthur never even bothered to have the score published, with the result that the drama's music is now entirely lost, except for the song "Little Maid of Arcadee" and possibly "Climbing over Rocky Mountain" (whose lyrics, at least, would reappear none the worse for wear in *The Pirates of Penzance* nine years later). One problem with *Thespis* may have been the length of the ballads: The "Railroad Song" in Act I is five verses long, and the verses have thirteen lines each if you count the chorus. In subsequent operettas Gilbert's songs would rarely run to more than three stanzas.

It is a fact – so little known that it bears repeating here – that Gilbert himself was tone-deaf. Nothing was wrong with his sense of rhythm, however; Deems Taylor has astutely pointed out that corresponding lines of successive verses of a Gilbert song always have the same number of feet and identical stress pattern. (Gilbert said that several of the *Bab Ballads* were written to be singable, if not sung, to specific popular tunes of the day. But we digress.) Curiously, with *Thespis*, Gilbert did for the chorus the inverse of what Thespis was credited with doing for Athenian solo actors: Prior to Gilbert, the English stage chorus was a semianimate body with little more to do than had the props and backdrop. Gilbert turned it into an animate body with music and function of its own. One testy prima donna complained during rehearsals of being put through tiresome blocking: "Really, Mr. Gilbert! I am not a chorus girl!" "No, madam," replied Gilbert; "your voice is not strong enough, or perhaps you would be!" Gilbert also firmly reestablished the patter-song genre, traceable back to Aristophanes.

Aristophanes, undoubtedly the principal comic playwright of the fifth century B.C., wrote possibly as many as forty-four plays of which eleven have survived to the present. The three giants of Greek tragedy were unquestionably Aeschylus (525–456 B.C.), Sophocles (*ca.* 496–405 B.C.) and Euripides (*ca.* 484–406 B.C.). Aristophanes's *The Frogs* was produced shortly after Euripides's death; in it, he praises both Euripides and Aeschylus, but gives the palm to the latter because Aeschylus's *moral* virtue is greater. Both playwrights' ghosts are asked what to do about Alcibiades, and Aeschylus's shade answers, "Best not to rear a lion in the city; but if you do, best to yield to its ways." Curiously, Aristophanes makes no mention whatever of Sophocles, although all four men had produced plays for the same Athenian audiences (or their parents). Sparta does not seem to have gone in for public drama as distinct from ritual; possibly the Spartans were too busy bashing heads.

Of Aeschylus's sixty-odd ascribed plays we have only seven, including the *Oresteia*, the great trilogy on the murders in Agamemnon's household. Sophocles is said to have written over a hundred tragedies and satyr plays (bawdy burlesques inserted between tragic trilogies at the Great Dionysian Festival to break up the audience's *pathos* before the next onslaught; the actors strode around wearing immense leather phalloi, just to give you an idea). Of these, one satyr play and seven tragedies are still extant. Sophocles is best known for the *Oedipus* trilogy, but he, like Aeschylus, also wrote a play about Agamemnon's daughter Electra. (So did Euripides, and the three make an interesting boxed set.) Euripides's genius has been described (by the editor of *Chambers's Biographical Dictionary*) as "an unerring instinct for a 'situation'," as, for example, the tableau of Cassandra, Andromache, Hecabe, and the other widows of Ilium led captive in *The Trojan Women*. (This striking play probably failed to win the Dionysian tragedy prize in 415 B.C. solely on account of its pointed jabs at the Athenians' atrocious treatment of neutral Melos the previous year in the war with Sparta.) Sometimes Euripides sacrificed a plausible denouement to his love for situation, as when Athena appears at the end of *Ion* to smooth everyone's feathers; but nobody at Athens seems to have minded *very* much, not even Aristophanes, and Euripides's plays enjoyed considerable popularity in revivals a generation or two after his death. This possibly accounts for the survival of so many – eighteen out of a possible eighty or so – in comparison to the plays of his elder colleagues.

Other Greek playwrights, particularly of the Middle Comedy that followed the heyday of Aristophanes, are known to us in large part because Roman dramatists were inveterate borrowers and revived many of their plots. Some freely admitted it: Terence, in his prologue to *The Woman of Andros*, flatly states that he is taking scenes from the Greek plays *Andria* and *Perinthia*, both by Menander, adding, "Anyone who knows either of them knows them both, for their plots are very nearly identical." (Quintilian, in his *De Institutione Oratoria*, gives Menander very favorable reviews, and perhaps it is not too farfetched to suggest that Quintilian's pupil, Pliny the Younger, owes a great debt to the zippy dialogue of the Middle Comedy, and its Latin derivatives, in his own action-packed narratives, such as the account of the 79 A.D. eruption of Vesuvius in which his uncle, Pliny the Elder, perished.) Menander's work was almost unknown outside of secondary references until 1906, when a papyrus containing fragments of four different plays – some thirteen hundred lines in all – came to light in Egypt; but in 1957 the complete text of *Dyskolos* (*The Disagreeable Man*) turned up in a library in Geneva. Menander himself, born in 343 B.C., or a little over a century after Aristophanes, seems to have drowned in Athens's harbor, the Piraeus, at the age of sixty-six.

Terence, who was born a little over a century after *him*, died twenty years younger, but had already lived a full life. Born a slave in Africa, he gained first literacy (thanks to his master, the Roman senator Terentius), then freedom, then the friendship of Scipio Africanus the Younger and membership in his literary circle at Rome. Terence's *Phormio* is based on another Greek play, *The Litigant*, by one Apollodorus, about whom we know next to nothing. It was to be recycled by Molière as *Les Fourberies de Scapin* and, still later in England, as Thomas Othway's *The Cheats of Scapin*.

The *Medea* and *Oedipus* of Seneca (tutor to the young Emperor Nero and later a coconspirator in a plot to assassinate him) would have needed no attribution in their prologues, for the plays by Euripides and Sophocles on which they were based would have been as familiar to the educated Roman audience as *Macbeth* and *King Lear* are to educated audiences in the English-speaking world today. If by any chance it *did* all start with the elusive Thespis, we owe the fellow a great debt, no doubt about it.

Much has been said in praise of the physical plan of the Greek theater, so much, in fact, that it led a pioneer acoustical physicist, Wallace Sabine, to remark at the turn of the century that

the careful classical scholar, however gratified he may be by this praise of a notable Greek invention, regards himself as barred by contemporaneous evidence from accepting for the theater unqualified praise. . . . There is not a theater in Italy or Greece which is not in so ruined a condition today that it in no way whatever resembles acoustically its original form. If its acoustics are perfect today, they certainly were not originally.

Sabine concedes that the bowl-shaped amphitheaters with walls across the back of the stage could indeed carry the actor's voice to the rear seats better than open-air declamation from ground level to an audience seated around the speaker on a flat plain. Still, even with the wall behind him to reflect his voice, the Greco-Roman actor lost a lot of his energy up into the sky. Curiously, the megaphonelike mouthpieces in the tragic and comic masks would have had a tendency to exaggerate the *vertical* spread of sound (somewhat like a hi-fi tweeter) because the mouth slits were elongated in the *horizontal*; small wonder, then, if the megaphone masks were only occasionally used. The Roman architect Vitruvius suggested amplifying the actors by placing a series of inverted vases on tripods around the edges of the stage, which would vibrate sympathetically with various notes of the musical scale. This may possibly have been tried in some Greek theaters; but it would not have worked very well anyway since the overtones, not the fundamentals, convey most of the meaningful information in speech. Familiarity with the mythic plots from childhood, though, must have given the Greek theatergoer a leg up to understanding what was going on onstage, in a tragedy at least; and the judges at the Great Dionysian Festival almost certainly sat way down front.

Besides, any actor worth his salt – or salary, which in very ancient times would have amounted to the same thing – would have gone to some pains to enunciate his words clearly. (Had there been actresses in those days, no doubt they would have too – but apparently there weren't, the acting profession, like most others, having been sewn up by men.) Especially important to enunciate clearly would have been the "stop" consonants of Greek; *b, d, g; p, t, k;* and *pʰ, tʰ, kʰ.*

Greek *b, d,* and *g* were probably very much like our own (in "boy," "do," and "go"). These "voiced stop" sounds were represented by the letters *beta, delta,* and *gamma,* though in modern Greek, what with the vicissitudes of phonetic change, the sounds these letters represented in the classical language have all shifted to become spirants: *w* or *v* (actually a cross between the two); *th* (as in "father"); and a sound that defies description without reference to languages other than English – call it the consonant in Spanish *agua* or *hago,* or the voiced version of the *ch* of German *ach*. Modern Greek represents the "hard" *b*, *d*, and *g* sounds in the language by preceding *beta*, *delta*, and *gamma* by *mu* or *nu*, the letters for *m* and *n*, a clever orthographic device with much acoustic merit, since a spirant preceded by a homorganic nasal sounds very much like the corresponding voiced stop made at the same point of articulation.

The unvoiced stops of Classical Greek are a little harder to describe to the speaker of English, but we will give it a try. Classical Greek had two series of unvoiced stop consonants, the "unaspirated" series *p*, *t*, *k* (represented by the letters *pi*, *tau*, and *kappa*), and the "aspirated" series *pʰ*, *tʰ*, *kʰ* (represented by the letters *phi*, *theta*, and *chi*, all of which appear to have evolved from the Phoenician letter *teth*). The unaspirated stops were like the *p*, *t*, and *k* in English "spin," "stint," and "skin," while the aspirates were like the *p*, *t*, and *k* in English "pin," "tint," and "kin," the difference being that the aspirates were accompanied by a puff of air when spoken, while the unaspirated letters were not.

Speakers of English tend not to think about the difference between the aspirated and unaspirated stops in their language overmuch, since the distinction is a low-level phonetic one that doesn't reflect any differences in meaning. This was not so in Greek, however. *Térma* ("end, boundary") and *Thérma* (the name of a city in Aetolia noted for its hot springs, cf. *thermós*, "hot"), for example, were different words with different meanings reflected in their different pronunciations. Speakers of Greek as a second language were ridiculed at least as early as the time of Aristophanes for failing to make the distinction between the aspirated and unaspirated stops of the language, much as nonnative speakers of English who have difficulty distinguishing between the vowels in "meet" and "mitt" have been known to provoke politer native smiles when speaking of horses biting the bit or ghosts wrapped in sheets.

◄ I ►

IOTA

IS THE SMALLEST LETTER OF THE
Greek alphabet (if the not strictly alphabetic "rough"
and "smooth" breathing marks and the three accents
are discounted), just as *yod* was the smallest letter of
the Phoenician alphabet. As such, *iota* has come to mean
"the smallest possible something," as in "There is not
one iota of truth in what you have just said." English
jot, which comes via Latin from Greek *iota*, has a similar
sense, though originally the word meant the mark of
punctuation at the end of a sentence: Thus, "Not one
jot or tittle shall vanish from the law." (A *tittle* was a
comma, derived from Middle English *titel*, "diacritical
mark," which in turn came from Latin *titulus*, whence
also English "title.") *Iota* could refer in Greek to both
the minuscule and the infinitesimal.

The question of the infinitesimal interested the Greeks
no little. Although matter was reckoned as having a
smallest and finite subdivision, the atom (literally, "un-
cuttable"), thought experiments had no such restriction.
Zeno of Elea (born 488 B.C.), a disciple of Parmenides
who taught that Being is one and unchanging, contrived
a number of paradoxes all dealing with the relation of
the finite to the infinitesimal (and most of which, thinly
disguised, show up in Flann O'Brien's *The Third Policeman*, one of the most fiendishly funny books ever written
in English). Perhaps the best known of Zeno's paradoxes is that of Achilles and the Turtle: Achilles, the
semidivine hero of the *Iliad*, and the Turtle engaged
each other in a foot race. Since the Turtle was clearly the
slower of the two, he (or she) was given a slight handi-
cap. If space is seen as an infinite continuum of points,
infinitesimally close to each other, and Achilles must

pass through each point that the Turtle has passed through, Zeno argues that Achilles can never catch up with the Turtle, since when Achilles reaches any given point that the Turtle has passed, the Turtle will already be on the way to the next. Similarly, Zeno claimed to show that an arrow can never logically reach its intended target, since it must pass through an infinity of infinitesimally close points in space remaining stationary, however briefly, at each one, an idea which perhaps eventually helped spawn Newton's calculus.

Zeno was the first recorded master of the *reductio ad absurdum*, the demolition of a premise by carrying it to its logical (but impossible) conclusion. Aristotle, who had essentially the same commonsense notion that we do of time and space as continua of smaller segments, said that Zeno's paradoxes were fallacies, though he was hard put to refute them. And Seneca, Nero's tutor, once testily remarked, "If I accede to Parmenides, there is nothing left but the One; and if I accede to Zeno, not even the One is left."

The problem was not so much that the Greeks had figured out it was logically possible to bisect any straight line – spatial or temporal – between two points, even if they were infinitesimally close together. It was that they were easily beguiled into thinking that a person (or turtle or arrow) was somehow obliged to pause and rest, however briefly, at each point along the journey. The assumption is excusable enough, given the Greek preoccupation with equality and things equal from a logical point of view.

The Greek word for "equal," *ísos*, is preserved in a wide variety of English terms, some old and some new. An *isosceles* triangle is one with two sides of equal length (from *ísos*, "equal" plus *skélos*, "leg"). (The Romans get equal time with their term for a triangle with all sides the same: *equilateral*.) *Isotope* literally means "the same place, an equal place." (The same *top-* shows up in *Utopia*, a term coined by Saint Thomas More as a cross between *eu-topia*, "good place" and *a-topia*, "no place.") *Isotopes* are elements that occupy the same place in the periodic table of the elements, sharing common chemical properties but having different atomic weights (depending on the number of neutrons carried by each nucleus). Thus, for example, the ninety-second slot on the periodic table, uranium, is shared by three isotopes, U^{235}, U^{236}, and U^{238}. All three isotopes form a regular chemical compound, uranium hexafluoride; but whereas U^{236} is stable, U^{235} tends to shed subatomic particles and decay into plutonium, with pyrotechnic results. Again, carbon normally occurs as carbon^{12}, but there is always a predictable, though small amount of carbon^{14} around in the atmosphere as well. By comparing the amount of carbon^{14} left in a sample of organic material – say, the wooden pilings of the prehistoric lake settlements in Switzerland – with its known concentration in the atmosphere and its observed half-life, archeologists can date such findings to within a hundred years or so. Indeed, the decay rates of a number of radioactive isotopes are valuable clocks for archeologists, palaeontologists, and geologists, from the relatively short-lived carbon^{14} to the very long-lived U^{238}.

Other *iso-* words include *isobar* and *isogloss*, both being lines drawn on a map. An *isobar* (from *ísos*, "equal" and *báros*, "weight") is a line on a weather map connecting places with the same barometric pressure; an *isogloss* (from *ísos*, "equal" and *glôssa*, "tongue, language") is a line on a dialect map dividing the speakers of one region from another according to their pronunciation or linguistic usage. Thus, for example, a linguistic map of New England, New York, and Pennsylvania might show isoglosses separating the speakers who call a sandwich made with a long roll and cold cuts an "Italian sandwich" (Maine) from those who call it a "submarine sandwich" (Massachusetts), a "grinder" (Rhode Island and Connecticut), a "hero" (New York City), or a "hoagie" (Philadelphia). Sensitivity to isoglosses goes back to very early times: The residents of Gilead in biblical times used the *shibboleth* test on anyone they felt might be a spy, *shibboleth* ("sheaf of grain") being their pronunciation of the word that people on the other side of the isogloss customarily pronounced *sibboleth*. Similarly, during World War II, suspected draft evaders, posing as returning Canadians, were asked at the border to recite the alphabet as quickly as they could, the trick being to see whether they would say "zee" or "zed" for the last letter.

Like most Westerners, the Greeks seem to have felt that there was something inherently satisfying about equals, and especially about things that could be divided into two equal parts. Things that could not be divided into two equal parts were not so good, a notion that most Western languages underscore in their words for the "odd" and "even" numbers. The Greeks termed the odd numbers from three up – one was not considered odd – *perissós*, "extraordinary, strange," much as we call them "odd." Even numbers, on the other hand, were called *ártios*, which also meant "equal." (Compare the Latin words *par*, "even, equal" and *impar*, "unequal, odd.") *Ártios* seems to be related to the verb meaning "to fit together," to the Latin word *ars, artis*, "art," and possibly to the Sanskrit *ṛta*, "right, correct." The Persians were similarly enamored of dualities and things divisible by two: The state religion under Darius was Zoroastrianism, in which the world is seen as a grand staging ground for the contest of the forces of dark and light, good and evil, equal and opposing deities. This strong official policy of viewing the world in black and white may be said to have provoked an opposite and equal reaction by the followers of Islam, who hold that if one must choose between the two, the odd numbers are actually better than the even ones: Allah is One, and the odd numbers are in harmony with the One, while the even ones are decidedly out of step.

The Greek distinction among one, two, and many (even or odd) was reflected in its very grammatical system: Nouns were declined and verbs conjugated in the singular, dual, and plural, in line with the original Proto-Indo-European system. Thus: "All chariot drivers are liars (plural) except you and me (dual), and sometimes I wonder about you (singular)." Fine lines could be drawn, as in the opening lines of Xenophon's *Anabasis*: "Of Darius and Parysatis were born two children: the elder, Artaxerxes, and the younger, Cyrus," in which the verb *gígnontai* is in the plural rather than the dual, thus implying that Artaxerxes and Cyrus were not the only offspring of this marriage made in Persia. Indeed, Parysatis bore Darius a staggering thirteen children all told. How they ever managed the old "you cut and I'll choose" routine so popular among modern, two-children families, for dividing goodies into equal parts is a mystery, though mostly the solution seems to have been, then as now, the palace coup, winner take all.

Eventually, the dual as a grammatical category evanesced, throwing its lot in with the plural. Traces of this rare Indo-European delicacy may still be spotted on the lips of most modern speakers: Any arbiter of linguistic good taste will tell you in a trice that "strictly between you and me and the lamppost" is bad English and that what one should say is "strictly *among* you and me and the lamppost," the idea being that *between* is for one-on-one relations, while *among* is for the masses.

"Idea," "ideal," and "idol" all come from the Greek verb *ideîn*, "to see, know, appear," cognate with Sanskrit *vid*, "to know," Latin *vidēre*, "to see," and English "wise," the original w/v sound having fallen by the wayside in early Greek. "Idol" comes from the noun *eídōlon*, "image, phantom," a keystone of the Greeks' philosophical concern with the disparity between the real and the ideal. Plato probably put it best when he likened the perception of the ideal to shadows cast on a dark cave wall: The people inside the cave cannot see the light or the real world outside the cave, but they can construe reality (albeit imperfectly) by watching the moving shadows. Saint Paul offers a similar view of the world in I Corinthians 13: "For now we see through a glass darkly [we look into a clouded mirror], but then face to face [but that's as "real" as it gets]." The eye of the beholder has at least this much to do with the letter *i* – and more.

One version of the story of the Trojan War, allegedly precipitated by the abduction of the Princess Helen, says that she was actually whisked away not to Troy, the city everyone wanted to go to war with anyway, but to Egypt, and that she was replaced by an *eidōlon*, or phantom, which was what Paris actually took to Troy and over which the Greeks fought for ten years. *Idolatry*, or an overweening interest in *icons* (or *ikons*, "likenesses") was – and continued to be – a matter of some argument among the peoples of the eastern Mediterranean for many a year.

Nowadays, the term *icon* refers specifically to a picture or sculpture of a saint or of Jesus Himself. In the Byzantine Church, and the Russian Orthodox that grew from it, icons have played an important part in daily worship: Saint Athanasios of Alexandria, noting the relationship in a portrait of the ideal to the real, says that the picture itself, could it speak, might say: "The emperor is in me and I in him; I and the emperor are one." This notion was given drastically short shrift by the Byzantines' next-door neighbors, the followers of Muhammad, who went so far as to say that *all* representational art was sinful, in that it smacked of worship of other than the one true (and unrepresentable) reality, God. The Byzantines were undaunted: As Basil the Patriarch put it, "The honor bestowed upon the icon is bestowed upon the prototype."

Despite a period of *iconoclasm*, literally "image-smashing" (a reaction within the Byzantine Church to presumed excessive idolatry in the eighth and ninth centuries A.D., no doubt in part as a result of the influx of Islamic ideas), the veneration of icons continues to this day in the Eastern Church. In traditional Russian homes, for example, the icon has a special place of its own. It is greeted by every visitor on entering the house and is turned to the wall when couples are making love in the same room.

◄ 𝕂 ►

KAPPA

IS FOR A WHOLE SLEW OF WORDS IN
English that are generally written with the letter *c*:
center, Corinth, cycle, circle, circus – these last two via
Latin – and *cylinder*, to mention only a few. The reason
why these words all begin with *c* in English is that the
Romans, from whom we got our alphabet, never had
much use for the letter *k*, preferring to represent both
their "hard" *g* and *k* sounds with their version of the
Greek *gamma* (Phoenician *gimel*, whence our word
"camel," after whose shape the letter originally took its
name). Although the Romans eventually borrowed the
letter *k* too, they used it only very sparingly, almost exclusively for words lifted directly from Greek, like
kalends (whence our "calendar" with its Latinate *c*).
Many of the *c* words mentioned above had already found
their way into spoken – and written – Latin before this
relatively late addition to the Roman alphabet.

Center is from Greek *kéntron*, which originally meant
"ox-goad, pointed stick." Eventually its meaning was
generalized to cover any pointed thing, such as a spur,
quill, peg, or the stationary point of a compass or divider,
hence the center of a circle. It is this last sense that
underlies the English word with its myriad shades of
meaning. Actually, there are two English words, "center"
and "center," one of which is from Greek *kéntron* and
the other of which is from Latin *cingere*, "to gird
about," as with a belt, whence also English "cinch." This
latter "center" is a structural engineering term, and
designates the wooden frame on top of which an arch is
built, supporting the arch until the keystone is put in
place.

Corinth (Greek *Kórinthos*) was the name of the city

situated on the narrow isthmus that joins the Peloponnese to the Greek mainland. The Corinthians had a reputation for luxuriant living, no doubt a deserved one, since they were admirably well-placed to engage both in sea trade with the Adriatic and the Aegean and in what little overland mercantile traffic there was between the Greek mainland and the Peloponnese. Plato, in *The Republic*, specifically mentions the Corinthian prostitutes as people to be excluded from the ideal state, thereby offering a gloss on at least one aspect of the local economy. The Corinthian style of column capital, with its ornate leaf pattern, is the fanciest of the Greek Big Three, the Doric being stepped at the top, and the Ionic having a simple scroll motif. Corinthian vases were prized in Rome and commanded a high price: at least one Roman emperor was said to have murdered certain senators for their collections, if the sometimes fanciful Suetonius is to be believed. (Even if he isn't, it still makes a good story.) And, long after the city of Corinth had slipped from prominence, the dapper youths of upper New York State at the turn of the last century were locally known as "Corinthians," according to Samuel Hopkins Adams, a testimonial to their financial and social well-being – and to the trend in American aesthetics called "Greek Revival."

Cycle is from Greek *kýklos*, which meant "ring, circle, wheel," though it also came to be used figuratively in the sense of "an epoch or era" and "a collection" of poems or songs. All of these meanings, with the possible exception of the first, have been carried over into English. We speak of song and sonnet cycles and, somewhat redundantly, of *The Ring Cycle*, Richard Wagner's operatic tetralogy, *Der Ring des Nibelungen*. People *used* to speak of a cycle of years, and if they no longer do so, it is perhaps only because of the rapid acceleration of time in this modern age of technological and political revolution. Or perhaps the cycle of years has simply been replaced by the mechanical cycle, such as is found in the two-cycle engine and the sixty-cycle alternating current that infuses everyday electrical appliances. Nor should we neglect to mention the -cycle of *unicycle*, *bicycle*, and *tricycle*, marvelous inventions all, the words themselves being no less marvelous inventions, exhibiting a Latin prefix and a Greek suffix. Finally, let us not forget the astronomical cycle, the circular path described by a celestial orb, such as the earth around the sun. In this last case, astronomers nowadays prefer the term "orbit" or "year," though the term *epicycle* is still in use when it comes to talk about the pre-Copernican cosmology of Claudius Ptolemy.

Ptolemy (100–178 A.D.), a Greek scientist born and bred in Alexandria, is remembered to this day as the ingenious elaborator and exponent of a view of the universe that has the earth at its center, immobile, around which all the other heavenly bodies turn. Basically, the idea was this: The universe was a hollow sphere to whose circumference were attached the stars. The earth was suspended at the center of this sphere rotating in a westerly direction once every twenty-four hours, give or take a few minutes, with Polaris, the North Star, the center of its apparent axis. The sun, moon, and the known planets of the day (Mercury, Venus, Mars, Jupiter, and Saturn) orbited or "wandered" around the earth in a more or less easterly direction, much, as Vitruvius put it, like ants on a moving potter's wheel marching against the spin. (The word *planet* comes from the Greek verb *planâsthai*, "to wander"; the sun and the moon were considered to be planets on the same order as the others.) All well and good.

The difficulty was this: If you watch the planets carefully, as Ptolemy and many of his predecessors had, they sometimes appear to slow down (relative to the "fixed" movement of the stars), stop, back up, and then resume their original course. This apparent phenomenon was termed "retrograde motion" and was a very popular point of discussion with the local astrologers, in those days the largest underwriters of astronomical research and development. Ptolemy managed to account for this fly in the celestial ointment by proposing the notion of the *epicycle*. Instead of merely moving around the earth in circular orbit, as had previously been thought, each planet was now hypothesized to be traveling in a circle (an epicycle) around a central point, which was itself traveling in a circle around the earth. (This latter orbit was called a *deferent*, from Latin *dē*, "from, away" and *ferre*, "to carry.") By fudging a little with the number of rotations that a planet seemed to make around this central point for every rotation of that point around the earth, Ptolemy was able to describe, and to predict, planetary motion in such a way that those who knew what he was talking about – mostly the astrologers – were satisfied and could go about the business of casting "accurate" horoscopes for centuries to come in perfect confidence, which is not to badmouth the astrologers. They were among the best and most serious scientists of their day; though many of their basic assumptions have by now fallen into disrepute, this is a fate shared by much of the ancient world's best scientific thinking. Ptolemy's hypotheses about the universe, as recorded in his treatise, *Hē Mathēmatikē Syntáxis* ("The Rational Putting-It-All-Together"), was sufficiently well-respected by the Arabs of the early Middle Ages that when they translated the work into Arabic, they gave it the title *Almagest*, "The Great One."

The troubles began a good thousand years after the first appearance of Ptolemy's *Syntáxis*, when it became increasingly clear that the movements of the planets predicted in the work simply didn't jibe any longer with what people could see with the naked eye. For several centuries, astronomers tinkered with the system, as scientists do when they have a theory that they think is basically okay, adding epicycles to epicycles to explain each new celestial wobble that came to light. The system finally came to be so ponderous and ungracious, with its unwieldy baggage of epicycle upon epicycle, that people began to suspect that God in His infinite wisdom couldn't possibly have created a system so complex, even on a bad day.

So it finally fell to Nicholas Copernicus, the Polish scientist and cleric, to say in the introduction to his *Dē Revolutionibus Orbium Caelestium* (*Concerning the Rotations of the Celestial Orbs*), published in 1543, that

the mathematicians are so uncertain about the movements of the Sun and the Moon that they cannot describe, let alone explain, the constancy of the length of the seasonal year. . . . Some talk about homocentric circles, . . . others about eccentrics and epicycles . . . but they have all been unable to see the principal thing: the shape of the universe and the invariable symmetry of its various component parts.

The purely aesthetic grounds on which Copernicus rejected the Ptolemaic model of the universe should not be underrated. As Thomas Kuhn has pointed out in his landmark book, *The Structure of Scientific Revolutions*, often the sheer complexity and unwieldiness of an outmoded theory drives the young Turks of the scholarly world to reject it in favor of a newer, shinier model, even if that newer, shinier model still hasn't had all of the bugs worked out of it yet.

Such was the story with Copernicus's novel proposal, which actually wasn't as novel as all that, since others well before him had suggested that the universe could just as well be a nongeocentric system. Pythagoras of Samos in the fifth century B.C. had suggested that everything in the sky spun around a central fire (to which humans somehow managed to have their backs perpetually turned, which accounted for their inability to see it); and Aristarchos, also of Samos, conjectured some two hundred years later that the sun was in fact the center of the whole shebang, with the earth and the other planets circling around it. So, perhaps there is nothing new under the sun after all, though this was hardly the reaction to Copernicus's book when it first came out.

It is perhaps impossible for a twentieth-century reader to imagine the intensity of the emotional storm Copernicus's *Dē Revolutionibus* generated in the literate European community, particularly in Roman Catholic circles. While Pope Paul II, to whom Copernicus had respectfully addressed the preface to his earth-shaking work, took no particular notice of it, perhaps because he never troubled himself to read it, the Church did eventually (in 1616) outlaw the teaching that the sun was the center of the solar system. However, the first and fiercest critics of the book were the Protestant divines – most notably John Calvin and Martin Luther's chief disciple, Melancthon. (And while the name of Melancthon may not be on the tip of too many tongues these days, it was not so very many months ago that the authors spotted this fresh graffito on the wall of a public house in one New England college town: "Calvin was only fooling," a wonderful piece of youthful wishful thinking if ever there was one.) Even Copernicus's publisher saw fit to include a preface (albeit unauthorized) by the Lutheran luminary Andreas Osiander, who, in an attempt to smooth the feathers he knew full well would be ruffled by the book once it was in hand, took pains to stress that what followed was only a *model* of the cosmos, after all, and that astronomers need not believe a word of it, though they *might* use the book to obtain accurate research results, heh, heh.

Modern introductory textbooks to the fields of astronomy and astrophysics more than occasionally begin with a similar disclaimer, asking the student to imagine the universe as though it worked in the way that Ptolemy said it did, with the earth in the center, and all that, so as to get ready to learn a less intuitive but more reliable way of looking at everything. Of course, the real kicker was that Copernicus's many charts and tables weren't much better than Ptolemy's when it came to describing or predicting anything, though this was never actually the issue. The real problem was that, while on the one hand, the old theory that Copernicus's work purported to refute was cumbersome and clumsy, on the other, the new theory raised some serious questions of theology: If the earth, instead of being the center of everything, were merely another planet in the vast whatever, why should God ever have troubled Himself about us, making the earth the particular staging ground for Adam's fall and man's redemption? Wasn't Copernicus going flat against Holy Scripture?

This was no empty question. Galileo, who died ninety-nine years after the publication of Copernicus's revolutionary work and who was the first earthling ever to see the moons of Jupiter through his ingenious invention, the telescope, punched the final hole in the doctrine of the immutability of the heavens. For this, he spent the rest of his life under Inquisition house arrest, though by this time, the religious authorities in both the Catholic and Protestant churches were fighting a losing battle. Although in 1611 John Donne could grumble that the "new Philosophy calls all in doubt/. . . men confess that this world's spent,/ When in the Planets, and the Firmament/ They see so many new," most astronomers had already accepted the new, heliocentric cosmology, or something like it.

It would be nice if *circle* were related to *cycle*, but it isn't. *Circle* comes from Latin *circulus*, the diminutive of *circus*, "circle, ring," which, once *circulus* had been coined, also came to have something of its modern-day meaning. *Circus* (which, incidentally, also gives us the word *search*) seems to have come into Latin from Greek *kríkos/kírkos*. Liddell and Scott gloss *kírkos* as "a kind of hawk or falcon which flies in wheels or circles – as omens were drawn from its flight, it was sacred to Apollo; a kind of wolf; a circle, ring, but usually in the form *kríkos*." *Kríkos* is glossed simply as "a circle, ring." In English, *circus* still maintains its original sense of "circle, ring" as in "three-ring circus" and, in British English, "Picadilly Circus" and the like, referring to circular traffic intersections.

Cylinder and its close cousin, *calender* (a machine that presses fabric, paper, etc., between two or more revolving cylinders), *are* related to the word *cycle*, harking back to a verbal root meaning "to roll." The other kind of *calendar*, while ultimately from Greek, is another story entirely.

The *Kalends* was the first day of the Roman month (and later came to be used in the sense of "month"). *Kalends* comes from the Greek verb *kálein*, "to proclaim," the idea being that the first day of the month was something worthy of announcement. (The other big days of the Roman month were the *nones* – the ninth day – and the *ides* – the fifteenth.) Since the Greeks didn't make any particular fuss over the first day of the month, "at the Greek Kalends" was a Roman expression meaning "never": "I'll pay you back on the Greek Kalends," i.e., when hell freezes over.

LAMBDA

IS FOR *LOGOS*, "THE WORD" (AS IN, *En archê ên ho lógos*, "In the beginning was the Word"). Actually, "word," or even "The Word," is a woefully inadequate rendering of this term in English; and, indeed, no native speaker of Classical Greek would have been caught dead using *lógos* for "word" in the strictly grammatical sense. For this, they would have used either *épos* (whence English "epic") designating "the spoken word," or *rhêma* (whence English "rhetoric"), referring primarily to the word as a spoken entity, with the secondary meaning of "verb." (*Rhêma*, though it may not look it on the face of things, comes from the same Indo-European root for both "word" and "verb," the initial *w* or *v* sound having been lost in Greek in the normal course of linguistic events.)

Lógos, rather, referred simultaneously to the outward expression of a concept, as opposed to a mere name, *and* to the actual concept itself. Thus, what there was in the beginning, according to Saint John at least, was a combination of the thought and its verbal expression, not just the one or the other. Many languages like to keep these two things – the idea of a thing, and the word for it – distinct at all times. Latin makes the distinction in its words *ratio*, "the thought" (whence English "rational" and "ratiocination," a five-dollar word for "thinking, reasoning") and *oratio*, "the expression of thought" (whence English "oratory"). For the Greeks, *lógos* in grammar meant "sentence" (which we get from Latin *sententia*, "opinion, way of thinking, sense") – the expression of a complete thought. *Lógos* could also be used in Greek to refer to reasoning itself: That which is *logical* is "thought out" or "reasoned." Other meanings for the word *lógos* include "that which is said; a saying; a fable, story; a referent, thing spoken of; a proposition, principle; an explanation" – you get the idea. (And if not, Liddell and Scott have two and a half good, solid columns of dense print devoted to the meanings of *lógos* in their *Greek-English Lexicon* to which the utterly insatiable reader is directed with our blessings. Liddell, incidentally, was the father of Alice Liddell, the "Alice" of *Alice in Wonderland*.)

Lógos is the noun that goes with the Greek verb *légein* (cognate with Latin *legere*, no less pregnant with meaning, its primary sense being "to read"). *Légein* seems to have meant originally "to gather, pick out, choose," a sense still in evidence in some of our Latin-derived words, such as *delegate* and *elect*, or the slightly more rarified *analect*, as in *The Analects of Confucius*, a careful selection of the sage's works. Nor should we overlook *dialectic*, the process of argument moving from thesis, to antithesis, to what each arguer hopes will be the unequivocally logical synthesis of the discussion. Subsequently, *légein* also came to mean "to speak, argue, reason" and, perhaps most significantly, "to read (aloud)." From the verb *légein* comes the noun *léxis*, which meant both "word" in the usual sense and also "manner of speaking" (whence English *dyslexia*, an umbrella term for disorders of both speaking and reading). It is this sense that persists in the word "dialect," *dialégein* meaning "to talk with, argue with someone" or, more specifically, "to speak in (a Greek) dialect."

A distinction should be drawn here, too. Barbarians, whom the Greeks considered to be anyone who couldn't speak their language, were not able to *dialégein*. Rather, they babbled, for want of a better word. The Greek word for "babble" also, as it happens, begins with *lambda*: *lálein*, which appears in English in a number of technical terms, such as *glossolalia*, "speaking in tongues," the *glosso-* being Attic dialect for pan-Greek *glotto-*, "tongue," as in *epiglottis* and, in certain dialects of

English, the "glo"al stop"; *lalophobia,* "fear of speaking," lest one bobble it, or, more specifically, "fear of stuttering"; and, via Greco-Roman scientific talk, *Homo alalus,* an early humanoid ancestor of us all who, presumably, could not even babble, let alone parse a Greek verb, calling to mind the famous boxing-ring cartoon captioned "My man don't fight until we hear it talk."

Dialect as a source of humor was already well established by the time of Aristophanes (late fifth to early fourth century B.C.) who used it with devastating effect when it came to putting words into the mouths of his Spartan characters for his Athenian audience of theatergoers. *Lambda* is also for "Lacedaemonian" or "Laconian," which is what the Athenians generally called their Spartan neighbors in polite company, the Spartan countryside being called Laconia. The Spartans, as immediate neighbors to the Athenians, were the stock people to make fun of in Athens, partly because of their different habits and view of the world, and partly, one suspects, simply because they were there to be made fun of.

The Athenians spoke an Ionian dialect, like most of the eastern Greeks and the Greeks of Asia Minor, whereas the landlocked Spartans on the mainland spoke with a decidedly Dorian twang. In English translations of Athenian theater, Spartan speech is often rendered in Scottish brogue: Thus, Aristophanes's Lacedaemonians are forever swearing "Be the twa Gads," i.e., Castor and Pollux. The Athenians enjoyed a great many boff-yoks at the expense of their close Lacedaemonian-Spartan country cousins, especially when they were at war with them (which was relatively often). The Athenians prided themselves not only on their high-class pronunciation of the words of the language but also on the fact that Athens was a democracy (leaving aside the question of slavery, for the nonce, as well as their occasional fits of oligarchy and out-and-out tyranny as the governmental drug of choice); whereas, by contrast, the Spartan state was a monarchy – of sorts, with two kings – with a powerful military class bringing up the rear, heavily supported by the *helots*, who were little better than serfs when it came right down to it.

Spartan austerity has remained a byword to this day, the object of mixed scorn and admiration in its own era. Thus, the three hundred stalwart Laconians who fell holding the pass at Thermopylae against the entire invading Persian army had as an oft-quoted epitaph: "Tell them back home in Sparta that you saw us lying here in obedience to her laws." Yet at the same time, the story is told of Diogenes the Cynic who, on seeing some fops from Corinth got up in all their finery to see the Olympic Games, growled "Affectation!" and, spying some Spartans, who had also come to see the games, dressed in their austere, even shabby clothes, cried "*More* affectation!"

The Laconians were also celebrated for their pithy speech, and anecdotes about the Laconic style enjoyed the same sort of currency and character as our modern-day jokes about down-Easters and up-country Yankees, as "Have you lived here all your life?" "Not yet." Thus it was said that when one of Sparta's allies was under siege and envoys were sent to appeal to the Spartans for aid, the *ephors* (a council of five officials elected to keep the Spartan kings in line) replied to the envoys' impassioned speech by saying that the speech had been so long, they had forgotten the beginning of it and would the envoys please give them a précis? The enterprising envoys then came forward with a flour sack, turned it upside down, and said, "Our flour sack is empty," meaning that they had come to the end of their resources and wouldn't the Spartans like to help them out. "Ah," answered the *ephors*. And then after a pause, "But why didn't you simply say 'Empty'?" A variant of this hoary classic, current at the time, concerned a certain Spartan general who sent a terse dispatch home: "Thebes is taken," to which the *ephors* replied, "*Taken* would have sufficed." It is undoubtedly with a nod to the Laconic style that

Julius Caesar subsequently sent his *Vēnī; vīdī; vīcī* ("I came; I saw; I conquered") message back to Rome after his victory in Pontus.

The Laconians-Lacedaemonians-Spartans also had a reputation for penny pinching. A common tale had it that the inhabitants of Taenarum, at the very southern tip of the Spartan territory on the Peloponnesian Peninsula, dispensed with the customary *obol* in the mouths of their dead (to pay the ferryman to the world of the dead, much along the same lines as the old English custom of placing pennies on the eyes of the deceased), since a back way down to Hades was said to be in the vicinity, and the Taenarians figured that their loved ones could bypass Charon's ferry to the underworld and thus not need the money for the toll. Many modern equivalents may be found in Scots jokes such as, ". . . and what an *expensive* city Edinburgh was: Hadna been there but half a day and bang went sixpence!" or the one about the Scotsman who promised his friend to pour a fifth of whiskey over his grave, saying that he hoped it would be all right if he passed it through his kidneys first.

It is unfortunate that we have no surviving Greek joke books, though they must have existed, as attested by a number of later Roman sources that shed at least oblique light on the Greek comic tradition, from which the Romans drew freely. The great Roman comic dramatists Plautus and Terence both admit in the prologues to several of their plays to having shamelessly cribbed from Greek sources, as Shakespeare and Molière would later admit to having borrowed from *them*. Quintilian too, although primarily a teacher of courtroom rhetoric, devotes considerable space in his *Institutio Orationis* to an analysis of classical Greco-Roman humor as used by lawyers to liven up the proceedings when the magistrate appeared sleepy or bored and therefore likely to find for the other party out of sheer impatience and ennui. Quintilian distinguishes among a number of different types of humor current in Greco-Roman society: *Urbanitas*, "language with a smack of the city in its words, accent, and idiom [at which the fledgling *New Yorker* succeeded so well and at which many of its epigones so utterly failed] having a tincture of learning . . . the opposite of rusticity"; *venustus*, "that which is said with grace and charm"; *salsus*, "the salt of wit . . . about which there is nothing insipid, . . . a condiment . . . which stimulates our taste and saves a speech from becoming tedious." Quintilian adds that "Cicero said that all true wit [of the salty variety] came originally from the Athenians." He further suggests that humor can be classed, functionally, as being concerned either with things and people or with words – Laconian dialect jokes being a good Greek example of the former, and *paranomasia*, "punning" being an example of the latter.

One stock form of Greek humor recorded by Quintilian and other early writers on the art of the jest is the "pedant" joke, of which a fair sampling survive in a manuscript attributed to one Hierocles of Alexandria and entitled *The Golden Words of Pythagoras*. Although these stories were originally told about Pythagoras, who may or may not have had his head perennially in the clouds, at least one modern editor (P. M. Zall, in his introduction to the marvelous sixteenth-century jestbooks collected under the title of *A Hundred Merry Tales*) has observed that they are "derivative of a timeless tradition that attributes to some cultural or ethnic class the facility for blundering by taking everything literally and being completely impractical about matters of fact."

Modern equivalents are the Ashkenazic stories of the much-maligned Polish *shtetl* of Chelm, whose inhabitants are traditionally held to be incurably literal-minded and dense, or the Polish/Irish/Swedish/French Canadian/Italian/Welsh/etc. jokes of the English-speaking world, the particular ethnic group singled out for ridicule constituting a sizable – though not *too* sizable – minority.

As in how many Poles/Irishmen/Swedes/French Cana-
dians/Italians/Welshmen/etc. does it take to change
a lightbulb? Eighty-seven: one to hold the lightbulb
and eighty-six to rotate the house. Why is the Polish/
Irish/etc. suicide rate so low in Chicago/Boston? Well,
have you ever tried to kill yourself by jumping out
a basement window? Or, in the Midwest, where there is
a large population of both Swedes and Norwegians, a
story is told of the native who sold his outhouse to a
Swede for an exorbitant sum and, inquiring of him later
how he was enjoying his new home, is given the following response: "Oh, I like it very well; I've rented the
downstairs to a Norwegian." Substitute any ethnic group
for another according to the demographic composition of
the region and the ethnic background of the teller, as
was surely the case in ancient Greece and, quite possibly,
in the even smaller and more parochial world of the very
first cave dwellers. Who knows?

Although Quintilian is wary of what he terms Cicero's
coarseness, it is unquestionably so that a great deal of
both Greek and Roman humor was strictly of the
slipping-on-the-banana-peel, Boston-cream-pie-in-the-face
school. Aristophanes, as a prime example, has his male
characters cavorting about sporting the traditional Dionysian leather phalloi (as did his literary heirs in the
commedia dell'arte centuries later) incorporating these
grotesque props most notably in his earthy antiwar
effort, Lysistrata. Here he has the envoy from Sparta
arrive to sue for peace with Athens (since Lysistrata
has persuaded the women on both sides to withhold
their favors from their menfolk until the war is over).
"Are you a man or are you Priapus?" ask the Athenians; "Or do you hide a lance under your cloak?"
"It's no lance; it's my dispatch case," retorts the obviously very horny Lacedaemonian to undoubtedly rafter-
shaking laughter on the part of the discerning audience.
In another play, three Scythians – no constant friends of
the Athenians – foul their breeches in terror, one after

another. And in *The Frogs*, we have the guy-dies-and-goes-to-hell jokes in superabundance aimed at bringing down at least two of the "serious" literary types of the day:

Euripides: No man is in all respects happy. One nobly poor is needy / Another of low birth —

Aeschylus: — finds his oilcan empty. (Har har.)

Homosexual innuendo is also played for a laugh: In *Lysistrata*, again, one of the men complains that "unless peace is soon declared, we shall be driven / In the void of women to give Cleisthenes a tumble."

But even though the letter *lambda* has recently been revived in America as a symbol for gay power, there are, to the best of our knowledge, no Lesbian jokes.

Λλ

◄ M ►

M U

IS FOR *MYTH, MINOAN,* AND *MYCE-naean. Mŷthos* to the Greeks meant "something passed on by word of mouth" and, by extension, "a legend, a tale." It is the latter sense, of course, that has been retained in English, often with a pejorative aftertaste (as in: "Dr. Jones, by dint of a decade of painstaking research, has definitively exploded the myth that trout live in trees"). While it is difficult (without mythologizing) to make a blanket statement about the general attitude that the Greeks took toward the stories we now call "the Greek myths," this much is certain: Much of what has been learned about preclassical (preliterary) Greek history from the paleolinguistic and archeological researches of the past century has shown that the early Greek mythmakers were not just spinning idle yarns. A lot of the stuff of the Greek myths turns out, perhaps not altogether surprisingly, to have been based on actual events.

The first and foremost source for Greek myth and legend is the pair of eighth-century B.C. masterpieces, the *Iliad* and the *Odyssey,* attributed to the blind poet Homer, mythical himself but who may have in fact existed. He is said to have come from Ionia (Greek-speaking Asia Minor), though a popular round has it that "Seven cities of Greece 't is said/ Claimed Homer's birth when he was dead/ Through which, in life, he begged his bread." Others have said that there was no single poet involved in the authorship of these epics, that Homer, the sole author of the *Iliad* and the *Odyssey,* is a fiction. Maybe so. In any event, until the end of the last century, historians tended to snigger at Homer's gods, monsters, miracles, and magic, dismissing all but his most barefaced historical assertions: That the ancient

Greeks knew something about sailing, that the folks on the mainland and the folks in Asia Minor had certain differences, that they all wore bronze armor when it came down to a fight, and that, once upon a time, there was a city called Troy.

Enter Heinrich Schliemann, a brilliant – or extremely lucky – self-starter in the latter part of the 1800s, an era in which luck and brilliance seem to have enjoyed a particularly felicitous relationship. The entrepreneurial Schliemann set out to sea to seek his fortune in his adolescence, passing the dreary hours on ship by teaching himself a number of languages. His method was to memorize a text in the language that he wished to learn – he is said to have learned English by memorizing great gobs of Sir Walter Scott – and to test his new-found knowledge with the closest person to hand who claimed competence of some sort in the language in question. As a result, Schliemann's command of phonetics was no great shakes, but he did doggedly acquire a good reading knowledge of several languages, among them Classical Greek.

Having amassed a quite considerable bankroll by his various mercantile endeavors, Schliemann was finally able in his early middle age to turn his full attention toward the fulltime pursuit of his first love: the heroic history of ancient Greece. Firmly convinced of the reality of Troy and its mythological trappings, he set off to discover the actual city; and lo and behold, he did. By a singular stroke of good fortune, he and his band of amateur archeologists hit upon the right spot on the first try, the hill called Hissarlik on the Scamander River, roughly three miles south of the river's mouth at the Aegean end of the Hellespont. This site had been overlooked prior to Schliemann's arrival in 1870 because classicists had generally supposed Troy to be another four miles to the south, where ruins stood near the modern town of Bunarbashi. Excavating the northwest corner of the hill – or rather, supervising (with a pistol in his belt and a whip in his hand, according to one biographer)

the work crew of ten Turkish laborers – Schliemann uncovered traces of the first building in an hour, and the
charred ruins of ten more buildings by the end of the
first day. (These proved to be the ruins of a much later
Troy, however, as suggested by a coin found in the
cinders and dating from the time of the Roman Emperor
Commodus, a vain athlete who was strangled by an
opponent in a wrestling match.) The excavation was
interrupted when the owners of the land, whose permis-
sion Schliemann had neglected to ask, showed up and
ordered him to cease and desist.

It took Schliemann a year and a half to get things
straightened out with the Turkish authorities, but by the
winter of 1871–1872 he was back at Hissarlik with a
hundred and twenty Greek workers, whom he promptly
fired en masse in a labor dispute and equally promptly
replaced. In June of 1872, almost two years to the day
from his first dig, he uncovered a magnificent Ptolemaic-
era bas-relief of Apollo in his four-horse sun-chariot. This
he immediately arranged to have smuggled out of Turkey
to Greece, where it stood in the garden of Schliemann's
house in Athens for some years thereafter.

The following May, Schliemann's crew found six bas-
ketfuls of gold artifacts, a hoard, with typical confidence,
he instantly pronounced to have been the treasure of
King Priam, "that mythical king, of a mythical city, who
lived in a mythical heroic age," as he liked to say when
speaking of it later. This treasure, too, he smuggled out
of Turkey, reburying it in several lots back in Greece,
anticipating – rightly – the diplomatic storm that would
break between Greece and Turkey when his discoveries
were announced. The following year he began to dig
at Mycenae, with the Greek government's guarded ap-
proval, as the Turks brought suit against him for the
value of the missing Hissarlik hoard. (They were eventually awarded 50,000 francs – about five cents on the
dollar – and went away seemingly satisfied.)

Schliemann's archaeological methods, shared by at

least some of his contemporaries, were not above re-
proach. "He is eagerly demolishing everything Roman and
Greek in sight in order to lay bare the cyclopean walls,"
complained Stamatakes, the representative from the
Greek Archaeological Society appointed to supervise
Schliemann's Mycenaean dig. In September of 1876,
Schliemann found his first gold artifact (a button) on the
site at Mycenae; by winter he had excavated several tombs
rich in treasure, including a number of curious gold
death-masks, one of which he promptly declared to have
been that of the mythical King Agamemnon.

The Trojan treasure Schliemann left to the German
people on his death, where it was housed in a special
wing of the Berlin Völkerkundemuseum until World
War II; it was then moved to a bunker under the Berlin
Zoo for safekeeping. The entire collection disappeared
behind the advancing Russian lines in 1945. The Mycenaean treasures remain in Greece – the famous death-
masks may be seen at the National Archaeological Mu-
seum in Athens. In 1888, three years before he died,
Schliemann attempted to get a dig going at Knossos, the
site of the palace of the mythical King Minos in Crete;
but shady dealing by the owners of the land – and Schliemann's hot temper – caused the negotiations to break
down irreparably. It was left to the ultimate purchaser of
the land, Sir Arthur Evans, to uncover the ruined Minoan
capital in 1900.

The Minoans seem to have been non-Indo-European
invaders, possibly from the Nile Delta, though the evidence is by no means conclusive. Part of the difficulty is
that while one of the Minoan scripts, Linear B, was
finally decoded by philologist Michael Ventris in 1952,
the older Linear A is still mysterious, though recent
studies link it to Ugaritic and Hebrew. While the written
documents left by the Minoans tell us far less than we
would like to know, the wealth of Minoan artifacts and
the information that may be gleaned from them is considerable. It may safely be inferred that the earlier

Minoan culture flourished from around 3000 B.C. to just after 1500 B.C., at which time a catastrophe occurred and Crete fell to the Mycenaeans. At the height of their power, the Minoans had at least four sprawling palace complexes, with up to fifteen hundred rooms, surrounded by cities of up to eighty thousand souls, with highly sophisticated plumbing and drainage systems. The Minoans were a major maritime power and managed for some time to keep the Aegean relatively free of pirates. For sport, they had athletic events at which young men and women would execute somersaults and handsprings from the long horns of charging bulls.

Shortly after 1500 B.C., however, the Minoan civilization abruptly came to an end. It is not clear what caused the virtually simultaneous destruction of four of the great Minoan palaces (Knossos was destroyed some fifty years later), but one candidate gaining increasing support is the cataclysmic eruption of the volcanic island of Thera, seventy miles north of Crete, which is known to have happened at about that time. Akrotiri – the site of one Minoan settlement that overlooked the crater of the old volcano – has yielded relatively few movable artifacts of value, possibly because the inhibitants had plenty of time to evacuate the area; but the site contains some vivid frescoes of everyday Minoan life in an excellent state of preservation.

Another theory has it that the Minoan palaces were sacked and torched by invading Mycenaeans. We do know this: The Mycenaeans were masters of the Aegean and much of the Mediterranean from about 1400 B.C. to 1200 B.C. or thereabouts. They adopted and adapted the pictographic script of the Minoan Linear A and used it to write their early dialect of Greek in the syllabic script now known as Linear B. It used to be said, before its decipherment, that "the only thing certain about Linear B is that it's not Greek." (Something still said with obvious justification, is that the Greeks took *two* shots at alphabetic writing: The Minoans invented their syllabic system, or took it from the Near East, and passed it on to the Mycenaeans, who made it more phonetic but never passed it on. Then, later Greeks took the Phoenician outgrowth of the original Near Eastern writing system and made the alphabet out of it.)

We think we know at least a few other things: Mycenae and the other contemporary Greek city-states that came under Mycenaean rule were peopled by a mixture of dark-haired locals, greatly influenced by centuries of contact with the Mediterranean Minoans, and the ruling fair-haired Achaeans. The latter seem to have come on the scene from the north at about the time of the destruction of the Minoan palaces, and crop up in Hittite and ancient Egyptian literature as sea-raiding, border-skirmishing tough guys, rather like the Normans in more recent times.

The Mycenaean citadels of mainland Greece have city walls built of tremendous stones. The walls are called "cyclopean" because of the traditional belief that, being too great for men to move, they must have been put there by a cyclops or some other freelance giant. (The contemporary view of the mechanics involved in the building of the walls is congruent with the old wheeze about the family that moved its piano upstairs: "How did you do it?" "We hitched the cat to it." "The *cat*?" "Well, we used a whip.")

The Mycenaeans had bronze armor and, later, iron weapons, and were clever enough to build their fortified cities at the center of an elaborate network of intersecting roads, allowing rapid military transit and deployment. The Mycenaeans seem to have been content to remain dependent on the leftovers of the Minoan civilization for their nonmilitary culture, borrowing among other things the basic form of their writing system. (One contemporary archaeologist has characterized the entire extant corpus of the Mycenaean Linear B as "the contents of a few wastebaskets at five state capitals.")

On the other hand, the fusion of Mycenaean values and Minoan techniques produced some interesting hybrids: While the Mycenaean potters continued the use of geometrical ornament on their earthenware, they also began to portray human figures, which the Minoans had confined to fresco and metalwork. One Mycenaean warrior's bronze dagger is inlaid with a gold and silver scene of several armed men trying to kill a lion that has already knocked one of the participants in the fray to the ground. The death-masks unearthed at Mycenae by Schliemann (which date from about a hundred and fifty years before the fall of Homer's Troy) are masterful studies in death and transfiguration, portraits of kings become gods. One of these masks has a most enigmatic smile, as if the dying king had just been told the punch line to some cosmic joke.

It was the Achaean warriors who banded together in 1200 B.C. or so to sack the city of Troy – or rather, Troy VI, as it is known in the annals of modern archaeological research, since at least a dozen different cities were built, destroyed, and rebuilt on the same site. (Schliemann missed Homeric Troy almost altogether; his understudy, Wilhelm Dörpfeld excavated what was left of it – a house corner and part of a section of the fortifications – and reconstructed the sequence of Troys from his own work and Schliemann's notes.) Within a mere hundred years, the Achaeans themselves had been dethroned by another wave of invaders, this time, the Greek-speaking Dorians.

At that point, some of the Mycenaeans fled overseas to Asia Minor and became the Ionians, Homer's people. Back on the mainland, the Minoan-Mycenaean culture gave its last gasp: Homer himself credits not the Achaeans but the foreign craftsmen of Phoenicia for the various articles of luxury he describes in the *Iliad*, apparently in the belief that such sophisticated stuff could never have been produced by native Greek artisans.

So there things stood: The Minoans and the Mycenaeans were long gone, and it was a good three centuries between their passing and the flowering of culture that produced Homer and Hesiod – and written history.

N U

IS FOR *NEMESIS* AND *NUMISMATICS*.
The common source for the seemingly quite disparate
concepts expressed by these two words – "divine wrath
and retribution" and "money" – may be found, with a
little digging, in the verb *némein*, "to distribute, to
manage" and the related noun *nómos*, "that which is
distributed or apportioned" and, by extension, "a custom, law."

Némesis originally meant, simply, "the act of distribut-
ing or apportioning" and later came to mean "(divine)
wrath and retribution, righteous indignation at a breach
of the rules," the idea being, apparently, that the gods
were no less evenhanded in their meting out of punishment than their mortal counterparts, and *everyone* had
a good right to be annoyed at folks who went against the
grain. *Némesis*, with a capital N, was the personification
of divine wrath at wrongdoing, and the meter-outer of
punishment for those caught transgressing the social
order, much as *Éros* was the personification of carnal
love (and Cupid, in Roman times, was the personification of desire).

Nómos (and its dialectal variant, *noûmmos*) was the
inanimate embodiment of the distributive principle: It
was the custom, the law, the standard measure of behavior and of actual weight. With the advent of money,
it was money – an invention involving standard value and,
of course, the capability for literal distribution. A *nómos*
(*noûmmos*) came to mean, specifically, "a coin worth a
quarter of a *drachmé*." From this, the Romans derived
their word *nummus*, "coin of the realm, cash on hand"
and, later, "small, not terribly valuable coin," which they
used in expressions comparable to our "not worth a cent

(a nickel; a dime)," inflation being an early concomitant of a money economy. (The word *economy*, incidentally, also contains the Greek term *nómos*, the literal meaning being "management [*nómos*] of the household [*oîkos*].) *Nummus*, or one of its cousins, also gives us *number*, *numeral*, and *supernumerary*.

But back to *numismatics*, the study and collection of money. The development of money arises naturally enough from a community need to store or transfer wealth other than in kind. Consider the plight of the owner of seventy-three cows who wants to liquidate his (literally *pecuniary*) assets (*pecunia* being the Latin word, first, for "cattle," then "money" in general, whence English *impecunious*). If all the would-be merchant can get for his seventy-three head of cattle is a quantity of some similarly bulky natural commodity – say, a thousand boatloads of fish – he is going to have a very hard time indeed running around trying to convert this wealth into property (never mind pass it on to his grandchildren on his shuffling off this mortal coil). The obvious but by no means inconsequential drawback of a barter economy is that you have to do an awful lot of legwork for what by all rights *ought* to be a relatively straightforward trans-action – converting the cows into fish, fish into wheat, trading the wheat for horses, swapping the horses for swine, and so on until you come up with just the right stuff in the appropriate denominations to conclude the deal with the person who has the goods you actually wanted in the first place.

Innumerable stories, the world over, rest on the in-herent cumbersomeness of barter economy. Most of the tales of the Western world, at least, which involve some play on the problem, fall into one or the other of two major classes: The person who starts out with some-thing valuable and manages to barter it down to some-thing relatively worthless through inept trading; and the person who engages in an elaborate series of trades only to wind up with precisely the same thing that he or she started out with in the first place – a sort of zero-entropy story. Stories of the first sort generally seem to be more popular: The simpleton receives a huge weight of gold as payment for several years' service and on the way home successively trades it for a variety of farm animals, until he winds up with a millstone, which he ultimately discards by the roadside because it's too damned heavy to carry the rest of the way home; or he is sent to market with the family cow and winds up dragging a pound of butter home on a tether; and so on. (The latter story, whatever its actual provenance, has a protagonist with a Greek name in its standard Western recension.)

The first Western-world steps toward a real money-based economy from a purely barter system seem to have come with the appearance of "tool money"; certain tools commonly in use whose general utility was commonly known came to be accepted as currency of a more or less customary value – worth more where the tools and the technology behind them were new or the materials for their manufacture were scarce or unknown, and less where everybody made his own as a matter of course. In colonial and federal America, powder and shot passed as currency since England had pursued a deliberate policy of keeping cold cash out of the hands of the colonists to the extent possible. Samuel Hopkins Adams, writing after a century of independence, reports that his grandfather, who briefly managed a circus in upstate New York in the early 1800s, accepted powder, shot, plug tobacco, eggs, and other equally worldly goods in lieu of monetary ad-mission to the show, drawing the line only when a prospective customer slapped a well-cured scalp down on the counter and wanted in. Axheads were used in both Europe and the Americas in early times for trade. In Greece, the iron spit (*obolós*) introduced from the north became a standard unit of currency in precoinage times, along with the *drachmé*, equal to six *oboloí*. Both the *obolós* ("obol") and the *drachmḗ* ("drachma") appear, with a faint pre-Indo-European tarnish, in the Greek system of coinage.

Precious-metal coinage seems to have come from Mesopotamia and spread, first, to the northwest. Originally, gold and silver ornaments were exchanged, with sales reckoned by count ("tale, tally") rather than by weight. This practice survives even today in the trading of at least some commodities, though, then as now, certain assumptions are made about the quality (and the weight) of the enumerated goodies. The earliest recognizable coins among the Greek-speaking world – and the West in general – come from Lydia in Asia Minor. (The Lydians, while in constant close contact with the Greeks, were apparently non-Indo-European in origin and spoke Greek only as a second – or third or fourth – language.) The Lydian coins date from the eighth or ninth century B.C. and are of electrum, a mixture of gold and silver. (Croesus, the last king of Lydia, began to switch the country to a gold currency in the middle of the sixth century B.C.) Metal discs excavated from early (1300 B.C. or so) Crete might have had some monetary use, but were more probably ornamental. The first clear-cut minted silver money on mainland Greece comes from Aegina in about 750 B.C.

Other Greek cities soon picked up on the idea of easily negotiable precious-metal money, and such coinage rapidly replaced the older and more unwieldy barter and iron-tool economies. Nevertheless, the names of the old units of trade stuck, at least as far as the obol and the drachma were concerned, as did the old ratios of value: six to one. Larger units were also coined: The *mnâ*, "mina" (worth 100 drachmas) and the *tálanton*, "talent" (worth 60 minas) both had definite, agreed-upon values in weight – how else could it be used for trade out in the boonies (not to mention in the rest of the so-called civilized world)? (The modern reader, living in a really civilized world, in which money is all so much paper, may read and weep.)

The talent had a consensual weight of a little over fifty pounds. And there was no fooling about it: A talent of silver was supposed to be just that, namely, fifty-six-odd pounds of silver. Naturally nobody lugged around coins of that size, just as most of us don't go walking around with thousand-dollar bills in our pockets. Generally, coins of considerably smaller denominations were used. In the more prosperous and economically active parts of ancient Greece, smaller denominations were struck and handed out as wages, the largest in general use in the fifth century B.C. being the *tetrádrachmon* or four-drachma piece. However, in some places *only* large-denomination coins have been found, archaeological evidence that money as such was strictly for heavy business among the high rollers and the average working stiff still got paid in chickens, granola, and warm handshakes.

Solon of Athens is undoubtedly best remembered for his wise and humane recodification of the laws – *nómoi*, in contrast to the harsh edicts of the tyrant Draco, called *thesmoí*, "laws laid down." Economists, however, remember him chiefly for his cagey innovation of coining sixty-three hundred drachmas from a talent of silver (instead of the usual six thousand), thus making a 5 percent profit of three hundred drachmas per talent. This incidentally insured that the coins would be less likely to be taken out of circulation and melted down for their actual value – now slightly less than their face value – for sale to silversmiths.

It should be noted here that the relationship of silversmiths to governments involved in coinage was, until relatively recent times, an intimate if not downright incestuous one: Witness the regulations raising the flat- and hollow-ware standard to better than 95 percent fine in the late 1600s in order to discourage decirculation of the not-so-fine coinage at the time of the founding of the Bank of England. Or, again, the selection of Boston silversmith John Hull by the Great and General Court of Massachusetts to coin the Pine Tree shillings, the first indigenous New England money since wampum: Hull was the only man in town who had the necessary skills in assaying, refining, die cutting, and stamping to do the job properly.

Not all of the Greek city-states followed Solon's practice of quiet devaluation of the currency, however, with the result that, by the time of the Peloponnesian War, the drachma varied anywhere from 4.3 grams (Athens) to 6.0 grams (Aegina). The discrepancy was due to Athens's heavy involvement in the war, while Aegina stayed relatively out of the fray; also, Athens had very little in native silver deposits, while Aegina had silver to spare. War contracts surviving from this period are very careful to specify whose drachmas were to be used to pay the troops and suppliers of matériel: The Athens-Argos treaty of 420 B.C. fixed the rates of payment for troops on loan from one ally to the other at "three Aeginetan obols a day for a hoplite, archer, or peltast, and an Aeginetan drachma a day for a cavalryman."

An average day's wage for an artisan was between three obols and a drachma a day; Athenian jurors were paid two obols a day up to 425 B.C., and three obols a day thereafter. This sheds some interesting light on Jesus's parable of the Ten Talents: The conservative third servant with the smallest sum was actually entrusted with something like the equivalent of forty years' wages, so it is small wonder that he was reluctant to lose it in speculation. Again, Socrates and his friends, in proposing that he cop a plea and pay a fine of thirty minas instead of being put to death, were volunteering in effect to lay out a sum equal to ten or twenty years' hire for a fair-to-middling tradesman, hardly a token offer of restitution to the state.

Eventually, silver currency proved too cumbersome for large transactions, and so gold made its appearance as a standard of currency, gold being roughly fifteen times as rare as silver. (The known rarity of precious metals is the chief thing that makes them good bases for currency, with their properties of ductility and malleability running a good second.) Philip of Macedon, father of Alexander the Great, established a bimetallic standard with the ratio of silver to gold at one to ten. Prior to that time, almost all gold coins Greeks knew and loved were imports from Asia Minor. The Lydians, as mentioned previously, struck hard-currency coins of electrum, an alloy of gold and silver in roughly equal proportions. Electrum is harder than silver or gold alone, just as bronze, used by the Romans in their coinage, is harder than either of its individual constituents, copper and tin. But devaluing of the alloy by mixing in more cheaper metal than valuable soon proved good reason to go to a more uniform (and more easily verifiable) metallic base, in this case, gold. After the fall of the kingdom of Lydia under Croesus, the conquering Persians recalled all the outstanding electrum currency and, continuing a process begun by the defeated king, issued new coins of nearly pure gold, called "darics" after Darius, the Persian king. These coins weighed approximately a quarter of an ounce and were the substance of the pay that Cyrus the Younger gave Xenophon's Ten Thousand in their mercenary campaign against Artaxerxes. The Persians set *their* gold-to-silver ratio at 13½ to 1.

We are indebted to the Greeks for the first European stirrings of banking and monetary theory. Aristotle – Plato's pupil and Alexander the Great's tutor – wrote a treatise called the *Oeconomica* (*Economics*, or "The Home-Owner's Guide to Money Management") in which he explains the necessity for money as "serviceable for future exchange; it is the sort of security which we possess that, if we do not want a thing now, we shall be able to get it when we want it." He goes on to say that "money is a sort of medium or mean, for it measures everything and, consequently, measures, among other things, excess or deficiency, for example, the number of shoes which are equivalent to a house or a good meal." For Aristotle, the relationship between *nómos* the measure and *nómos* the coin was self-evident.

Banking in Athens seems to have arisen easily enough from the money-changing function of the temples. (This was to prove true somewhat later in Rome as well: *Juno Monēta*, Jupiter's wife, was, among her other claims to fame, the patron of the mint at Rome, located in her temple on the Capitol. Rome seems to have owed somewhat less to the Greeks on this particular score than to the Carthaginians, whose silver currency preceded that of Rome and from whom the word *monēta* seems to have been borrowed – whence our words "money" and "mint.") The Greek money-changers, operating out of the temples with their relative security, were known as *trapézitai* (from *trápeza*, "table") for the tables on which they weighed and transacted their business. It is their tables, or their Near Eastern counterparts that Jesus is said to have overturned at the temple in Jerusalem; though money-changing in a sacred (and secure) place, foreign as it may have seemed to the Jews, was not only familiar but officially sanctioned by the Greeks. The temples in their various cities initially merely facilitated monetary transfers between cities, much in the manner of our modern armed guards who appear at the factory on payday to cash the blue-collar worker's paycheck for a small consideration; they later came to accept deposits and lend money, in the manner of our modern-day banks. Accounting, however, remained in a primitive day-book form, with records of cash-in and cash-out in order of occurrence. Double-entry bookkeeping of the sort used in this day and age originated in the Renaissance in Venice.

The Athenian drachma, weighing about the same as a modern American quarter, was a little chunkier and bore the image of a wide-eyed owl, a totem animal sacred to Athena Parthenos, patron of Athens. Other cities issued coins with their own local gods or early corporate logos on them. Only after the death of Alexander the Great did somebody hit on the idea of putting a person's face on a coin; from there, it was hop-skip-and-a-jump to coinage bearing the noble visage of the local living ruler. The political and public-relations benefits of this last leap forward in coinage are clear enough; and in the case of devalued currency, the faces on the coins also served to indicate the purity of the metal, especially as successive rulers, following Solon, routinely revalued the currency when it came their turn to issue new money. This practice is still with us, witness the egregious example of the issue of the minuscule Susan B. Anthony "silver" dollar to replace the Eisenhower cartwheel.

K S I

IS FOR *XENOPHOBE, XERXES,* AND *XEN-ophon.* The Greeks' attitude toward foreigners was at best ambivalent. On the one hand, *ksénos* meant "strange, foreign; stranger, foreigner"; and, on the other, it meant "guest" or "visiting fireman," carrying with it the implicit reciprocal obligation to treat the stranger well when he was under your roof and to provide for his sustenance and safety. Thus, a *xenophobe* (from *phóbos,* "fear,") suffers from fear of, or a morbid aversion to, strangers or foreigners: much the same thing back then, one supposes, and perhaps – who knows? – the early Greek version of "the man who came to dinner." Whatever one's personal feelings might have been toward strangers, foreigners, or guests, there were strong prohibitions against turning the guest-friend or potential guest-host away from your door: Zeus Almighty would give you a hard time if you were inhospitable, as in the myth of Baucis and Philemon whose unfriendly neighbors he summarily turned into a nice lake.

The Greeks were not alone in the ancient world in (a) not caring that much for the arrival of strangers and (b) feeling nevertheless some obligation to look out for them if pressed, an ambivalence reflected in the double edge of the Golden Rule, "Do unto others as you would have them do unto you." The English word "host" tells it all: it concurrently means "a receiver of guests," "an army (of strangers)," and "the consecrated bread consumed in Communion." The first sense derives from Latin *hospes, hospitis,* "someone who receives strangers into his home" (whence also *hospital, hostel, hospice, hospitable,* and *hospitality*); the second, from Latin *hostis, hostis,* "stranger" and, later, "public enemy" (whence *hostile*, though Latin *hostis* is also cognate with English *guest*); and the third, from Latin *hostia*, which Ernout and Meillet in their *Dictionnaire étymologique de la langue latine* define as "a victim offered to the gods as an expiatory offering to appease their anger," and which they take pains to distinguish from *victīma*, "a victim offered in thanks for favors received." *Hostia* also gives us the word *hostage*.

As far as the early Greeks were concerned, *real* foreigners were people who didn't speak some recognizable dialect of Greek – *bárbaroi*, "babblers" (whence English *barbarians*). *Barbarians* were seen as something less than human. Their very presence could pollute the environment: after the Greek victory at Platea, all domestic fires were extinguished because the oracle had told the conquerors that these fires had been contaminated by the Persian invaders. The Greeks then rekindled the fires from the sacred flame on the altar at Delphi, just to be on the safe side.

Whether visiting *bárbaroi* were supposed to be accorded the same degree of hospitality as Greek-speaking guests is not clear, but it's a good bet that more than a few Greeks would have said, "Show me a barbarian who can parse a Greek verb – no mean feat – and I'll show you a human being." But the Greeks, despite their native caution and fundamental ethnocentrism, had an insatiable curiosity about the foreigner's exotic folkways. Herodotus devotes page upon page to the customs of the Scythians and other outlanders; and, true or not, such tales were eagerly devoured by the literate and illiterate alike. (Naturally, *some* of the information that Herodotus presents in his histories was grounded in fact – or personal observation, at any rate – and much of it was helpful as well as entertaining. And, too, there was a sense that if a barbarian *could* be taught to parse a Greek verb, there was always the possibility fruitful commercial relations might follow.)

On the other side of this coin, however, the practice of

xenelasy or *xenelasia*, at least on the part of the Spartans, should be mentioned: *Ksenēlasía* was, according to the Oxford English Dictionary, "a measure at Sparta for the expulsion of foreigners." The venerable OED goes on to quote the historian Grote to the effect that "Nor were strangers permitted to stay at Sparta; they came thither, it seems, by a sort of sufferance, but the uncourteous process called *xenelasy* was always available to remove them."

As the Greeks began to push their way into the Aegean and onto the mainland of Asia Minor, they came into increasing contact with a particular variety of barbarian-foreigner, the Persians, with whom they enjoyed an on-again, off-again (chiefly off-again) relationship from roughly 550 to 350 B.C. The story begins, to all intents and purposes, with the ascension of Cyrus the Great to the throne of the then rather small Persian kingdom in 550 B.C. He managed to subdue the Medes and the kingdom of Babylon, then controlled by the Chaldeans. Cyrus then moved his forces farther into Asia Minor, bringing to an end the rule of Croesus (as in "rich as Croesus"), king of Lydia.

Croesus tried to enlist the aid of the Spartans as well as that of the Ionian Greeks against the Persians and to some extent was successful in so doing, though there were some difficulties involving self-interest, prudence, and mutual distrust. He is said to have lost the war with Cyrus by a drastic misreading of the Delphic Oracle, who informed him that if he took the offensive against the Persians and crossed the Halys River, "a great army would be defeated." As it happened, the "great army" was not that of the Persians, as Croesus had assumed, but rather his own. With the fall of the Lydian kingdom, the littoral Greek states in Asia Minor also came under Persian domination.

Cyrus the Great was succeeded by his son Cambyses, said to be mad, who added Egypt to the Persian Empire and then promptly committed suicide. He was succeeded by Darius the Great in 522 or 521 B.C., after which time the Greek and Persian fur really began to fly. Darius took the wise precaution of dividing the then swelling Persian Empire into twenty satrapies or vice-royalties, putting members of his family in charge of the majority of them. Communications were handled by an elaborate system of royal highways and posthouses where horses and riders were stationed in readiness at all times. When a messenger rode in from, say, Babylon with a dispatch for the satrap in Sardis, a fresh rider took it and galloped off to the next posthouse, passed it on to the next rider, and so on down the line, until the message was delivered. The Greeks called such way stations *stathmoí*, "stopping places," from the verb *histánai*, "to stand," a *stathmós* being the distance reckoned by the Greeks as a day's march. The *stathmoí* were placed at roughly five-*parasang* intervals, the *parasang* being the Persian "league," though in rough terrain, they were closer. (The Greeks in the same era handled all *their* interurban correspondence by long-distance runners like Pheidippides, who ran the first marathon.)

The Persians were naturally proud of their ability to muster large forces quickly and deploy them effectively. Darius was eager to try these forces – which now included the remnants of the defeated Phoenician navy – against his neighbors to the west. This he did, marching across the Bosporus against the Scythians, who cut him off. He was saved by the Ionian Greeks, who preferred to fight for the Persians rather than ally themselves with their more hated foes. This alliance proved short-lived, for the Ionian states, backed by the Eretrians and the Athenian navy, soon revolted, and were promptly crushed.

A Persian expedition to punish the mainland Greeks who aided in this rebellion was mounted in 492 B.C., but ended in a massive shipwreck of the Persian fleet off Mount Athos. Two years later, with some inside help, the Persians once again set out to do battle with the Athenians. Led by Miltiades (in exile from the state of

Thrace), the mainland Greeks once again trounced the Persian forces. In a recurring scenario, the Athenians had tried to ally themselves with the Spartans, whom they didn't really like very much but whose superior land forces made a good, if unreliable backup to the Athenian navy. The Spartans were late in arriving at the crucial showdown, much to the displeasure of the stalwart Athenians and their Thracian commander.

Enter *Xerxes*, Darius's son and successor, and one of the more notable fellows. In 480 B.C., eight years after his succession to the Persian throne, Xerxes with his Ionian allies invaded Greece through Thrace and the northern mainland. He had come via Troy, where he had made a brief stop to sacrifice a thousand oxen and make a public vow of "revenge for the Trojan War." As the Persian fleet bottled up the Athenians and their some-time allies behind the island of Salamis, and having put the torch to Athens, Xerxes had his traveling throne set up on a promontory overlooking the bay, only to see his navy utterly wiped out. Early the next year, his army was soundly beaten at Platea, and Xerxes returned to Sardis much shaken and in some obvious displeasure. There he was murdered in a palace coup.

An inherent flaw in the Persian system of government was the inevitable power struggle among the satraps, particularly whenever the king died. Rival factions would each try to seat their man on the throne, pitting half-brother against brother, bastard son against legitimate offspring. As a result, there was rarely an orderly succession. Furthermore, once a new king was finally installed and the bodies of the other contenders were cleared away, he usually undertook a major bureaucratic reorganization. In the wake of just such a succession and bureaucratic shake-up, some sixty years after the assassination of Xerxes, Cyrus the Younger came to mount an army, largely composed of mercenary Greeks, against his brother Artaxerxes II (nicknamed *Mnemon*, "mindful").

On the death of Xerxes in 465 B.C., his son, Artaxerxes I (*Longimanus*, "long-handed") had acceded to the throne. He was followed by his son Darius II (*Nothos*, "bastard"), who, in turn, was followed by *his* son, Artaxerxes II in 404 B.C. or so. Ever "mindful," Artaxerxes II promptly did his best to forestall any overt expressions of sibling rivalry on the part of his brother Cyrus by relegating him to something of a back place in the empire. (He would in fact have killed him but for the timely intervention of his mom, the ruthless Dowager Queen Parysatis.) Cyrus's reaction to all of this was to go about quietly raising an army to tell his brother what for.

One of the Greeks who responded to the call (and the promised remunerations) was *Xenophon*, a literate young country gentleman. He was studying at Athens with Socrates when he received a letter from his old friend Proxenos the Boeotian, already at Sardis, promising him good pay, adventure, and an introduction to Cyrus himself. (By this time, it was no uncommon thing for talented Greeks to sell their skills abroad, even to the Persians. Not only did many of the Persian satraps routinely hire Greek mercenaries, but Greeks also served in Persia in the professions – Artaxerxes's personal physician was the Knidian diagnosticator Ktesias.) Xenophon accordingly left Athens (somewhat to Socrates's disgruntlement) and joined the ranks in Sardis. At full strength, Cyrus's forces numbered some 120,000 men, of whom approximately 13,000 were Greeks.

Cyrus marched the host forth, ostensibly on a punitive expedition against the rebellious Pisidians, but as the army drew farther and farther away from the coast and their real mission became increasingly unclear, the Greeks grew increasingly uneasy. Cyrus had neglected to tell his soldiers that he had in fact hired them for no less than a toppling of the present Persian regime. They finally dug their heels in and asked for both back-pay and a straight story about the actual military objectives of the campaign. Cyrus reluctantly tipped his hand, pacifying most of the troops by meeting – and bettering – their demands for pay. Unfortunately, by this time, the self-seeking satrap Tissaphernes had already warned King Artaxerxes of the plot afoot, so all was lost. Some fifty miles north of Babylon, at Kunaxa on the Euphrates, Cyrus and his troops were met by a royal force (led by none other than Tissaphernes) of an alleged million or more – "official" and "unofficial" estimates of troop strength and casualties were doubtless no more reliable then than they are today. In any event, Cyrus's army routed the king's men, though Cyrus himself was killed in the fray. Several days later, Tissaphernes, who must rank as one of the all-time bad guys of the ancient world, invited the Greek general staff to a peace parley and there slew them all.

This left the Greeks leaderless, far from home, and far from their best means of getting there, namely, over the water. And hopelessly surrounded by vastly superior numbers of a hostile foe. In typical Greek fashion, they elected a new commander: Xenophon. He graciously accepted this vote of confidence and proceeded to lead the retreating forces on the tortuous journey homeward, north along the Tigris, up into Armenia, and over the highlands to Pontus – a long and arduous forced march, under frequent fire, through most inhospitable terrain. It is to Xenophon's credit that better than eight thousand of the mercenaries survived to see the Black Sea. Unlike Balboa, "silent upon a peak in Darien," the Dorians who first reached the summit of Mount Teches went wild: *"Thálassa! Thálassa!"* they cried – "The sea! The sea!" The word went back down the column past where Xenophon was riding, and even the rearguard double-timed it up for a look. Everybody hugged and cried and kissed and danced around a huge cairn of stones, branches, and captured weaponry, surely one of the great tableaux of history.

Xenophon returned to Greece in time to enlist under King Agesilaos of Sparta; the Spartans by this time had grown disaffected with their alliance with Tissaphernes and declared war on him. Thus, a great many of Cyrus's Greek mercenaries got to do battle with Tissaphernes twice. Xenophon once again survived and retired to a fine estate near Olympia given him by Agesilaos for his many services rendered. There he devoted his time to hunting and to writing books, among these being his memoir of the Persian campaign, the *Anabasis* ("The March Up-Country"), and his recollections of Socrates, the *Memorabilia.*

All this is not to say that the Greeks had nothing but bad dealings with foreigners. They did, after all, receive the alphabet (or a first draft of it) from their maritime neighbors, the Phoenicians. *Ksi* started out as the Phoenician letter *samekh*, which represented a *sh* sound found in Phoenician but not in Greek. Not needing this letter for *s*, for which they used *sigma*, the eastern Greeks used it to represent *ks*. The western Greeks, whose alphabet underlies our own, used X (*chi* in the standard, eastern Greek alphabet) to represent *ks*, preferring to do without *samekh* altogether as a suspicious device of foreign invention.

◄ ◯ ►

OMICRON

(LITERALLY "LITTLE O, SHORT O," AS
opposed to *omega*, "big o, long o") is for *oenology* and
ornithopter. *Oenology*, the artful science, or scientific
art, of wine-making comes from the Greek word *oînos*,
"wine," a term of ultimately dubious parentage with
cognates in virtually all of the languages of the Mediterranean and the neighboring highlands. ("Wine," "vine,"
and the "vin-" of "vinegar" all come from the same
stock.) Whatever the origin of the word for wine, the
liquid was a staple and a major export product in Greece
well before the beginnings of recorded Greek history:
There is hardly a writer of prose or poetry from the time
of Homer onward who doesn't mention it glowingly.

The Greeks did not, by a long shot, invent wine.
Here, as in many other matters, the Egyptians were way
ahead of them, with wine jars dating from as early as
3000 B.C. and an admirably sophisticated system of label-
ing their contents by 1400 B.C. Wine jars from the time
of Amenhotep III, who straddled the turn of the fourteenth century before Christ, carried not only the name
of the region and vineyard where the wine was made and
the year – as French wines do to this day – but the name
of the supervising vintner as well.

Egyptian wine seems as a rule to have been on the dry
side, or so we might infer from the relatively small number of Egyptian wine jars bearing the notation "somewhat sweet," suggesting that "somewhat sweet" wines
were the exception rather than the ordinary fare.

The Greek contribution to oenological art was the
development of a wine that was strong, stable, and well-
packaged, thanks as much to the skill of the Greek
potters as to the vintners. After all, it is no big deal to

make a rudimentary wine: You mash up some sort of fruit, leave the mash to ferment, and pour off the liquid residue through a strainer when the process of fermentation has reached the desired point. Fermentation itself is the natural interaction of the yeasts that live on the skin of the mashed fruit with the sugars inherent in the fruit. The process of fermentation is self-limiting: Once the yeasts have converted a certain amount of the fruit sugars into alcohol, an environment is created that is too toxic for the yeasts to live in anymore, and even the strongest of wines peak out at an alcohol content of 15 percent (or 30 proof in modern parlance). At this point, the yeasts die off (presumably of cirrhosis of the liver) and what you get is vinegar if you wait a little longer, which is great if you like salads. The reason you get vinegar is that after the yeasts have fallen by the wayside in their drunken stupor, bacteria go to work, aided and abetted by local oxygen, to break down the products of fermentation. To combat this pernicious tendency, people eventually hit on the idea of storing their corked wine bottles flat, thereby assuring a liquid seal against the semiporous cork. But this was much later. The natural wines of the Egyptians and the early Greeks tended to be cloudy, weak, and unstable.

The Greeks discovered – probably from their Minoan cousins – that judicious pruning, careful cultivation of the stock, and supervised fermentation could produce a far stronger and potentially longer-lasting wine (if nobody swigged it down immediately) than the "natural" stuff. Homer attributes the ease with which Odysseus inebriated the Cyclops Polyphemus to the vast superiority of the Greek cultured wines. According to Homer, Zeus had set up the Cyclopes – the one-eyed ones – on an island Eden where everything grew in abundance and the grapes yielded wine, such as it was, right off the vine. But Odysseus's crew had earlier plundered the city of Ismarus and had carried off some of the best wine from the cellar of Maro, priest of Apollo. Maro's wine was said to be so potent that his housekeeper customarily diluted it twenty to one with water for everyday use. The unsuspecting, undiluted Polyphemus was under the table in no time.

Small wonder, then, that, gallon for gallon, Greek wine was considered a good buy all over the ancient world, especially given that it came in more or less airtight, nonporous Greek *amphorēs*, "jars." While the pharaohs' wines had all evaporated by the time they were unearthed by the intrepid archaeologists in the nineteenth and early twentieth centuries, Greek shipwreck sites have yielded stores of *amphorês* in more or less pristine condition, full to the brim with, well, vinegar. One can't after all expect miracles: The jars were not perfectly hermetically sealed, so a little oxygen must have crept in there, but the wine/vinegar was at least still uncontaminated by two millennia of surrounding seawater. So nearly airtight were the Greek *amphorês* that the Egyptians, according to Herodotus, used to save the empties and send them filled with water into the Syrian desert by caravan.

Dionysus was the Greek god of wine; his other name is Bacchus, that is, *bácchos*, "the raving one." Dionysus/Bacchus figures in one of the many god-dies-and-is-resurrected myths so popular in the ancient world. Cut into pieces by Hera (he was one of her husband Zeus's numerous illegitimate offspring), he was put back together again by his grandmother Rhea, and then kept hidden out of sight until his coming of age, much as Zeus had been. On reaching maturity, Dionysus was again smitten by the jealous Hera, this time with madness. This, however, seemed to suit Dionysus and his followers just fine, and the troupe of revelers rampaged their way through Asia Minor and Greece, with temples and altars being set up in honor of the new, mad god everywhere they went. Eventually the Olympians decided to acknowledge the *fait accompli* of his success, and Dionysus was offered, and accepted, a place at the gods' table. It is said this place was vacated by Hestia (Roman *Vesta*, of vestal virgins fame), who knew she could get a warm welcome (as goddess of the hearth) in any town in Greece she liked, and who was undoubtedly happy at the opportunity to escape the incessant bickering of her divine siblings. The Athenians venerated Dionysus in a number of ways, the most notable (and sober) being through the all-day drama contests held in his honor every year, which gave the world the Oedipus Cycle, the Oresteia, and the other great Greek tragedies.

The Athenians generally drank their wine diluted, except at breakfast. A play by one Alexis (*ca.* 350 B.C.) has a stranger ask the lawgiver Solon why the Athenians appeared to be such a sober lot, to which Solon replies, somewhat disingenuously, that the Athenian street sellers courteously premix their wine with water in order that the consumer might not be troubled by a hangover. It was the quality, in fact, and not the dilution of the Athenian wines that made for the proverbial *kraipalé Hellenike*, "Greek hangover" whose symptoms were a clear head and no headache the morning after, which is to say, no hangover at all. If Maro's wine was diluted with twenty parts water to one of wine for home consumption, of course, the strongest that it could conceivably have been was a working solution of ½ percent alcohol, or about one sixth the potency of domestic American beer.

Brandy (made by distilling wine) and sherry (made by distilling half the wine and then using that to "fortify" the other half) were both unknown to the Greeks. It is, oddly enough, to the officially teetotaling Arabs that we owe, if not the process of distillation itself, at least the word *alcohol* (as well as, for that matter, the word *sugar*). *Alcohol* (*al kohl*) originally referred to a powder, antimony sulphide, that was used in the Near East as eye-shadow and later came to designate any powder that could be purified by being vaporized and then condensed. The word finally came to refer to the liquid product of the process of distillation, as, for example, alcohol of wine (ethyl alcohol).

No treatise on the subject of oenology, however brief, would be complete without at least one joke involving the abuse of the grape: Two Athenian caterpillars, having spent the night in a not quite empty amphora, wobbled their way to the brim at the dawn's early light. As they reached the brim, they saw a butterfly flutter by, at which point one caterpillar mumbled to the other, "You'll never get *me* up in one of those things."

Many a sober citizen – and equally many a less-than-sober citizen – has said as much when confronted with the possibility of physical flight. But flight of fancy is naturally another story. Physical flight and flight of fancy dovetail nicely in the story of the *ornithopter*. An *ornithopter* (from Greek *órnis/órnithos*, "bird" and *pterón*, "wing") is a muscle-powered flying machine. Like perpetual motion machines, ornithopters have occupied the attention of many fine engineers for millennia, and, up until quite recently, with about as much practical success. After all, birds have a distinct advantage in flight over all other vertebrates by virtue of their hollow bones, giving structural support without much weight. Since the ratio between body weight and wing area (and therefore lift) is unfavorable for solid-boned creatures like ourselves, most experiments in human-powered, winged flight have been dismal failures.

Still, humans have remained steadfastly intrigued by the idea of self-propelled flight well beyond the perimeters of Greece. Most ancient cultures have their stories of winged gods, and Christian Westerners have their angels and witches. The best-known Greek contribution to the lore of human or humanoid flight is probably the story of Daedalus, who, great artificer that he may have been, wound up only batting .500 when it came to flight. Imprisoned by King Minos of Crete, he and his son Icarus set off to make good their escape with one pair each genuine, bird-feather-and-wax wings. Icarus unfortunately got carried away and flew too close to the sun, which melted his wings, depositing him with a resounding splash in the waters below where he drowned as a lesson to subsequent centuries of children who might otherwise have seriously considered disobeying their wise and prudent parents.

Other ornithopterous experiments have fared little better, though the Arab Armen Firman is said to have leapt from a tower in Córdoba in 852 A.D., braking his inevitable fall with a canvas cloak stretched on a frame – perhaps the first more or less successful parachute jump in recorded history. Twenty-three years later, a physician named Abbas bin Firnas was reported to have hang-glided for some minutes before seriously wrenching his back in a similarly precipitous landing. Indeed, the ninth king of Britain, Bladud (father of the more famous King Lear), who reportedly studied in Athens before coming home to assume the crown, died in the twentieth year of his reign (883 A.D.) attempting to fly – using the black arts – from the top of the temple of Apollo in London. *The Mirror for Magistrates* has him say:

> *Which learnéd, but not perfectly,*
> *Before I had thereof the sleight:*
> *I flew aloft but down fell I*
> *For want of skill againe to light.*

> *For what should I presume so highe,*
> *Against the cours of nature quite:*
> *To take me winges and saye to flye,*
> *A foole no fowle in feathers dight.*

(Peter Haining, in the introduction to his book on the history of human-powered flight, *The Compleat Bird-man*, recounts the story of one George Faux who, shortly after a well-publicized if somewhat ill-fated leap from the local alehouse roof, was heard to remark, "I'm really a good flyer, but I cannot alight very well.")

The refrain "If God had wanted men to fly . . ." became the prevalent sentiment among educated and laity alike, and generally remained so into the nineteenth century, despite occasional designs and experiments by such major lights as Roger Bacon and Leonardo da Vinci. The only people whose claims to flight were accepted at all in this time were witches, whose delusions, according to recent research, had their origins in the unwitting use of hallucinogenic yeasts and ointments, and whose powers (such as they were) were written off to demonic influences.

Although the Industrial Revolution reopened people's interest in all manner of technical feats long thought to be impossible, the best that anyone could do for the ornithopter was to invent (or reinvent) the hang glider. Otto Lilienthal was without a doubt the most successful at this, conducting meticulously recorded experiments in Berlin in the 1890s, though he himself lost lift and life when his hang glider crashed in 1896. Nevertheless, thanks to his notes and further study by the Franco-American physicist Octave Chanute, the Wright brothers were able to design and build working biplane kites by 1899, biplane gliders by 1902, and their motorized biplane by 1903.

From that point onward, most flight experiments were motorized, and the search for muscle-powered aircraft was all but utterly abandoned. Even though a British engineering firm established the Kremer Prize in 1952, a purse to be awarded to the first muscle-powered aircraft pilot to fly a figure eight around two pylons half a mile apart and clear a ten-foot hurdle at the finish, not too many people took the offer seriously; and so the money sat in a bank for twenty-five years accruing interest until the prize was worth some $85,000. Then, in 1977, the enterprising Paul B. McReady's "Gossamer Condor," an eighty-pound bicycle-powered glider, was successfully flown by a competition cyclist and part-time hang glider named Bruce Allen to win the Kremer Prize, and not long thereafter, with some modifications, the beast was flown across the English Channel, the first triumphant human-powered flight of any distance in however-many thousands of years of back-to-the-drawing-board.

We cannot leave the subject of physics and fancy and the letter *omicron* without at least perfunctory mention of *ontology*, that branch of metaphysics concerned with the true nature of existence. The physicist Albert Abraham Michelson, a sober fellow if ever there was one, on reading Einstein's early papers on the special theory of relativity, said that he admired the elegance of the mathematics but that the theory had "no ontological significance." However, the Michelson-Morley experiment – splitting a beam of light to measure its drift through the ether supposed, at that time, to exist between bodies in interplanetary space – not only proved the nonexistence of the hypothetical ether but provided unexpected support for Einstein's theory. Michelson refused to acknowledge the validity of the results, preferring to think that he had made a procedural error. Einstein, on the other hand, having a far greater respect for Michelson's laboratory technique than Michelson himself, at least in this instance, was overjoyed, naturally. (He may have allowed himself a celebratory glass of wine or two on the occasion, for all that; who knows?) In any event, Michelson never came around to the relativistic point of view, and indeed was said to have asked, in stentorian tones, whenever he entered the local cafe in which the physicists of the day met, "On which side of the room are the relativists, and on which side are the physicists?" so as not to sit, inadvertently, among the upstart crowd.

Bertrand Russell, one of the world's finer upstarts and fanciful flyers, reported that his grandmother dismissed metaphysics out of hand, noting dryly that the whole business could be summed up in two questions and answers: "What is mind? No matter. What is matter? Never mind."

PI

IS FOR *PALINDROME*, A WORD, PHRASE,
or, better still, a sentence whose written representation is
symmetrical in that the letters used to write the first half
are repeated in reverse order in the second. Examples
are: "Able was I ere I saw Elba," "Madam, I'm Adam"
(words of greeting addressed to the equally palindromic
Eve), and "A man, a plan, a canal: Panama!" *Palín*
means "back, again" in Greek and shows up in slightly
camouflaged form in the English word *palimpsest,* a
piece of paper with something written on it, on which
somebody has written something else; example: you run
into a friend and write her or his new phone number on
your newspaper or as-yet-unanswered letter from Mom or
the IRS.

Psên, whose past participle gives the *-psest* of *palimpsest,* literally means "to scrape, rub off": To write on a
previously besmirched piece of parchment, you had to
scrape the original ink off before you could write something new. To this day, the writers of books in Arabic
script, which persists in defying analysis into a small
enough number of components so that it may be typeset
with any ease, ask that scribal errors be "scratched out,"
as one would correct a ditto master with a razor blade.

"Interpolated palimpsests" are manuscripts filled between the lines with a second text. While these may be
a bit hard on the eyes and critical faculties, they don't
involve the number of blots and smudges of the true
palimpsest. Writers in Arabic script evolved a similar
convention: Books might appear with a text written by
one author in the center of the page, accompanied by an
often quite unrelated text by another author written in
the margins. This arrangement resulted in many an

author's bitter complaints about scribal error: "The verses of some son of a whore have crept from the margins into my deathless work," and the like. The essence of the problem was this: The *material* on which each author's deathless poetry or prose was written, by however careful a hand, was very valuable stuff indeed. So the literate were not above plundering whatever parchment or vellum was lying around and scraping it down for reuse or, if the original text was deemed too good to consign to oblivion, filling in the margins and the spaces between the lines.

The *-drome* of *palindrome* is the same one found in *hippodrome, aerodrome,* and *bowladrome* (a commercial neologism), and means "course, run." As a suffix of sorts, *-drome* may be attached to the name for virtually anything that runs or walks around a track, our favorite candidates for coinage being *otididrome,* an aviary for wild bustards – that staple of Xenophon's Greek mercenaries during one phase of their march up-country with Cyrus, and *philosophodrome,* a stately portico or colonnade where one can see the peripatetic sages sauntering about in weighty debate. Two other words in which *drome* already occurs are *dromedary,* the one-humped African camel noted for its prodigious running speed, and *syndrome,* a set of symptoms that appear together regularly in the course of a given disease.

Palindromic sentences were believed to have originated with a Thracian Greek named Sotades, which is why verses that read the same forwards and backwards are sometimes called *Sotadics.* Sotades was a sharp-tongued satirist who lived in the third century B.C. and is said to have met his untimely end when he wrote one too many about Ptolemy II, the second Greek king of Egypt, surnamed Philadelphos ("loves his brother"). Even brotherly love has its limits, of course, and Ptolemy, pushed beyond his, had Sotades kidnapped, sealed up inside a lead coffin, and unceremoniously heaved into the sea. Lest we be too harsh on Ptolemy for overreaction to scurrilous verse, there *is* an insult-to-injury quality about being lampooned both forward and backward at the same time.

Palindromes appeal to us, one suspects, because of their unusual symmetry. To be sure, this symmetry is by no means unqualified: The constituent letters of a palindrome are not necessarily reversible – if you hold a palindrome up to a mirror, the letters which are not symmetrical along their vertical axis will look funny – and if you read a palindrome into a tape recorder and then play the tape backwards, what you will hear will not only not be the palindrome, but eerie and inhuman-sounding gobbledygook, since human speech moves in one direction only: forward.

Some letters of the alphabet *are* symmetrical along their vertical axis – A, H, I, M, O, T, U, V, W, X, and Y, in our own – and many others, including *pi*, in Greek. Thus it would be possible to construct a palindrome in either English or Greek that was doubly symmetrical: It would read the same forward and backward *and* if held up to a mirror. (The construction of such a palindrome is left as an excrcise for the reader obsessed with orthographic symmetry.) Usually, though, the maker of palindromes is subject only to the constraints that the final product be reasonably intelligible and, when all is said and done, be composed of a string of letters that repeats in reverse order from the middle letter of the string.

Even the first constraint – that the message be reasonably intelligible – is subject to some fudging: Palindrome makers are allowed by convention to give a prefatory statement defining the context which would render the palindrome meaningful. Thus, "Napoleon said as he stepped off the boat carrying him to exile, 'Able was I ere I saw Elba'," (though he wasn't or he would still have been residing in Paris). Or, "As he came out of the divine anesthesia after the removal of his rib and saw that he had human company, Adam said, 'Madam, I'm Adam'." Or, "Here's a political slogan coined by Teddy

Roosevelt's speechwriters as he sought reelection to the presidency of the United States: 'A man, a plan, a canal: Panama'." (About which one United States senator in later years remarked, "Why should we give it [the canal] back to the Panamanians? After all, we stole it fair and square.")

The best palindromes need no such introduction or apology, stiff as they may sound without it. One of our personal favorites is "Lewd I did live & evil did I dwel," which is widely held to be the first recorded palindrome in English and is ascribed to John Taylor (1580–1653), sometimes called the "Water Poet." He composed it during the time that one could still get away with spelling "dwell" with a single *l* but well after the invention of the ampersand. Another favorite is "Pure Boston did not sober up," for which a variety of equally plausible contexts may readily be suggested.

Palindromes occur in other languages besides English and Greek. Dutch offers, among others, *Neder sit wort; trow tis reden* ("Words are paltry; it's the sense of what you say that counts"); and French has *Léon n'osa rêver à son Noël* ("Leon didn't dare dream about his Christmas," no doubt because he was due for a bundle of switches in his *sabot*). The French example is noteworthy, aside from its moral impact, because it contains all of the diacritics used in that language – acute accent, circumflex, grave accent, and dieresis or umlaut – all of which, like the distinction between upper case and lower case, must be ignored if the palindrome is to put its best foot forward.

The real masters of the palindrome are probably the Japanese, though neither of the two writing systems that the Japanese employ is alphabetic. One is a direct borrowing from the Chinese and is ideographic (one sign per word) and the other is syllabic (one sign per syllable), which, given the relatively uncomplicated syllabic structure of the language, works out pretty well. Consider the following palindromic poem (written in the traditional *waka* form of alternating lines of five and seven syllables) in which the syllable is the basic unit:

> *na ka ki yo no*
> *to o no ne bu ri no*
> *mi na me za me*
> *na mi no ri bu ne no*
> *o to no yo ki ka na.*

("The sleeping figure's eyes open in the middle of a winter's night – can it be in anticipation of the sound of the wave-borne boat?")

Symmetry pleased the Greeks, who had their own palindromes, such as, *nípson anomémata mē mónan ópsin* ("wash your sins, not just your face"). Indeed, the word "symmetry" comes from Greek *syn*, "with" and *metreîn*, "to measure," the idea being that if you measure half of an object with two equal parts, you have as much as measured all of it, since the whole thing is "all of a part." The notion that a device can be built in its mirror image and still work is an ancient, if not utterly reliable one.

Well, why not? The human body – "the measure of man" or, equally appropriately, "the measure of woman" – is from all outward appearances just about as symmetrical as you can get. Appearances are deceptive as often as not, though: It is a rare person whose two eyes are exactly even; and a nylon stocking the right length for one leg will seldom fit the other, a boon to the nylon stocking industry. People, furthermore, who talk or whistle out of one side of their mouths almost never are able to do so with equal ease on the other side. And there is always the problem of left-handedness versus right-handedness, with only the tiniest minority of the world's people able to claim genuine ambidexterity.

By and large, the world's technological inventions favor the right-handed. A common wood screw, for example, around which much subsidiary technology has evolved, has a right-handed thread, so that it will respond most kindly to being turned in the direction of the greatest torque, which a right-handed person is able to exert. (Much of this power is provided by a particular muscle at the base of the thumb that is quite useless when it comes to turning the screwdriver in the opposite direction. The next time you have to unscrew a tight screw, try doing it with your left hand, since the greater torque will be counter-clockwise. If you happen to be left-handed anyway, you're home free.) Because of this right-handed bias when it comes to making the threads for tightening things, some of the critical valves on, say, acetylene tanks are deliberately threaded left-handed. Again, scissors are usually designed for right-handed people. Left-to-right writing favors the right-handed also: The left-handed usually must evolve a slightly cramped writing posture to avoid dragging their sleeves in the fresh ink. And piano keyboards, with the treble on the right and the bass on the left, presuppose that one can play faster passages with one's right hand.

Under the skin we find that while our muscles and skeletons are symmetrical, our internal organs are virtually never so. True, pairs like the ovaries, testes (one of which, usually the left, habitually hangs lower), kidneys, and lungs are symmetrical, but the heart is neither symmetrical nor centrally located. Moreover, the whole alimentary canal is asymmetrical, as are the liver, spleen, gall bladder, etc. When medical examination finds these organs on the wrong side it is a likely sign that the patient was one of a pair of symmetrical identical twins.

Nor is the brain's activity symmetrical. The left hemisphere of the brain controls the right side of the body, while the right controls the left. However, the left hemisphere also houses the speech center. Researchers R. W. Sperry and Michael S. Gazzaniga found that in epileptic patients whose *grand mal* has been brought under control by the drastic operation severing the *corpus callosum,* the separated hemispheres seem to function almost independently. A pair of scissors would be shown to the right eye only; the right hand could then recognize the object by feel but the left could not. Again, when a picture of a naked woman was flashed to the right eye, the subject could readily say what he or she saw (note the behavioral asymmetry in postulating that a naked man might be offensive to one sex but a naked woman would offend neither). When the picture was shown to the *left* eye only, all subjects experienced a measurable emotional jolt but none could tell why ("that funny machine," was the best one subject could do): The right hemisphere "knew," but could not verbalize, what it had seen. (That either hemisphere can exercise control on both sides of the body, even after the split-brain operation, is due to the interaction of the motor paths in the brainstem and spinal cord.) Two questions worth further investigation are (1) whether symmetrically reversed twins have speech areas reversed to the right hemisphere and (2) what the neurological corollaries are to being left-handed (having the motor coordination of hand and eye predominate in the right hemisphere while speech and language are on the left).

Asymmetries abound in nature, too. One, the helix, occurs in many forms: Woodbine always spirals its way up a tree trunk in a clockwise helix, honeysuckle in a counterclockwise one. The double helix of DNA always coils in one direction. The path of the earth through space is in fact helical, for we orbit a sun that is itself moving relative to the other stars around us. Seafaring asymmetries include the flatfish who starts out life more or less symmetrical but in later life exhibits a truly wandering eye that migrates over to the other side of its head; and fiddler crabs have one claw a great deal larger than its opposite member. Symmetry seems a gift of nature sometimes withheld as if by caprice.

Aristophanes's speech in Plato's *Symposium* postulates that the original human beings had two heads, four arms, four legs, and so on. There were three sexes: double-man, double-woman, and man-woman. But Zeus cut them all in two when they tried to make war against him. "Love," Aristophanes goes on to say, "is the desire of bisected humans to return to their original form." Heterosexual lovers are descendants of the man-woman type, and homosexuals descendants of either double-man or double-woman. Aristophanes adds that Zeus threatens to bisect us all again if we don't behave, leaving us all to go hopping around on one leg. Here one is reminded of the Irish god Lir (father of Manannan, god of the tides), who had only half a tongue; consequently, when he gave orders for the construction of the universe, only half got built. Note: Isaac Asimov once demonstrated that one can always have half a cup of coffee but never half a piece of chalk.

Pi in and of itself is most familiar to modern readers as the symbol for the ratio of a circle's diameter to its circumference, an irrational number equal to 3.14159265358979. . . . Several clever mnemonics have been devised for remembering *pi* to *n* places, of which the cleverest is perhaps "God, I need a drink – alcoholic of course – after all those lectures exploring Quantum Mechanics." The number of letters in each word is the same as the number of each successive digit, an exercise not unrelated to the machinations of a clever palindromist.

RHO

IS FOR *RHETORIC, RHYTHM, RHYME,*
and *rhotacism,* all of which have more than a little to do
with the art of speaking. The fifth-century Athenians
were an intensely political people who loved a good
verbal knock-down-drag-out fight. They were forever
suing each other, if only for the opportunity to exercise
their rhetorical skills, and most of them managed to have
their say in court at least once in their lives. Since every
man was his own attorney and no one wished it to be
said that he had a fool for a client, the art of rhetoric
was soon refined to the level of science. It became part of
the standard school curriculum, where it remained en-
shrined well into the Middle Ages, with its division
of what every aspiring scholar should know into the
trivium – grammar, logic, and rhetoric – and the *quadriv-
ium* – arithmetic, geometry, astronomy, and music.

Everyone has no doubt heard how Demosthenes over-
came a weak voice and a stammer to become a celebrated
orator – local boy makes good – by filling his mouth with
pebbles and declaiming against the roar of the waves for
practice. A lesser known feature of the story is that
Demosthenes shaved off half his beard lest he be tempted
to return to polite Athenian society before he had had
plenty of time to complete these probably apocryphal
oral calisthenics. And what almost nobody remembers
(but is perhaps the most easily verifiable detail of the
tale) is that the prime reason Demosthenes had for un-
dertaking these verbal rigors was that he wished to go to
court to argue for the return of an inheritance out of
which he had been diddled by a fast-talking relative.
Whether the pebbles had something to do with it or not,
we cannot say, but Demosthenes did eventually get his

money back and went on to pursue an illustrious career as a public speaker and a writer of speeches for those whose dedication and native powers of persuasion were somewhat less than his own.

Indeed, many felt the need for tutoring in the art of friendly persuasion as they entered into not-so-friendly litigation with their fellow citizens. The Sophists soon rose to the occasion as specialists in and teachers of rhetoric, following their founding father, Protagoras, to whom is attributed the famous dictum: "Man is the measure of all things." (As a glance at a standard weights-and-measures table for English will demonstrate, Protagoras was perhaps prophetically correct: We speak of a *hand* when measuring the height of a horse; a *span* is the distance from the tip of the thumb to the tip of the little finger, conventionally reckoned at nine inches; a *foot* is a foot, and a *cubit* – from Latin *cubitum*, "elbow" – is the distance from the tip of your middle finger to your elbow; a *fathom* is the length of a rope which a standard-issue sailor stretches from one hand to the other across his back.) To Protagoras is also attributed the teaching that absolute truth – whatever that may have been or ever may be – was essentially unknowable, even when it came to the existence of the gods. "For the obstacles to this sort of knowledge," he said, "are many, including the obscurity of the matter and the brevity of the span of man's life."

The Athenians were, at least officially, a pious people, and Protagoras's casual view of theology did not sit well with them, if their public pronouncements are anything to go on. Many thought that Socrates was a Sophist, though he himself was at some pains to refute this accusation in the *Apology*, his defense in court as recorded – or fabricated after the fact – by Plato. What really incensed the Athenians, though, against the Sophists (and Socrates) was that their students seemed to have learned their rhetoric as much for the art of it as anything else and used their hard-won skills to unfair advantage in the courts, playing fast and loose with the actual merits of the case at hand, a familiar criticism to this day. After all, Socrates's pupil, Alcibiades, handsome and honey-tongued, had helped to ruin Athens by double-dealing with the Spartans, and Socrates was held to account for it.

The Sophists' pupils were forever being taken to task for cribbing their masters' speeches, whether they won or lost in court. While being coached by one's legal counsel was grudgingly admitted as fair play, having your lawyer ghostwrite your speech beforehand was definitely cheating, though not uncommon. Plato has Socrates say to Phaedrus, who has ostensibly come to discuss some arguments in an upcoming court case, "But first you must show me what you have in your hand hidden under your cloak, for that bulge, I suspect, is a draft of your actual speech; and, much as I love you, I am not willing to have you exercise your *memory* on me." Most of us feel that the distinction between off-the-cuff eloquence and prepared, previously rehearsed talk is a real one: "The senator departed from his prepared text to say . . ." is supposed to grab us in a way that a plain old, everyday speech is not, and in this we are merely following the Greeks, who felt that extemporized discourse was far better on the ears and mind than prefabricated fare.

The Sophists defended their position – that a speech prepared beforehand was perfectly okay – by arguing that good pleading made for higher truth, and given the absence of verifiable higher truths, that was the best that anyone could, or should, hope for. Plato, one of the greatest literary rhetoricians of all time, probably gives the Sophists a fair enough verbal shake when he has Protagoras say

Naturally, I don't deny that there is such a thing as wisdom or that wise men exist; but what I mean by "a wise man" is a person who can convince other people that what seems bad to them is actually good. Consider the case of the sick man whom the physician attempts to change into a healthy person. The aim of education is not so different from the physician's, namely: to change men from a worse condition to a better one. The only difference is that the physician brings about this change by means of drugs while the sophist does so by means of words.

Being paid to teach rhetoric, then, was no more unreasonable than exacting a fee for medical service, by the Sophists' lights at least. Indeed, their very name, *sophistikoí*, "knowledgeable ones" – their own term, it is only fair to say – made a special claim to professionalism: These were people competent in "knowledge" and in the skills of knowledge acquisition and the selling of these goodies to the uninitiated, not much different from carpenters or cooks. They knew their business, a valuable one, and they could teach it, heartily, for a fee.

This particular view of wisdom as a quantifiable commodity – whether we are talking epistemology (how a person should go about learning things) or "knowledge" as a relative thing – drew a lot of rhetorical fire not only from Plato and his Academy but from Aristophanes as well, though his potshots were aimed at Socrates and not the real *agents provocateurs*. Aristophanes's *The Clouds* is a classic farcical treatment of the relationship between litigant and teacher of rhetoric that has appeared in other oratorical trappings on the stage ever since.

Nevertheless, despite the jokes and criticism, some of the Sophists' pupils learned their lessons well and became good public speakers, and at least a subset of these may be presumed to have used their skills in the pursuit of what they thought was good and honorable. Demosthenes will always be remembered for his *Philippics*, the orations against the warmongering Philip of Macedon. And so will Pericles, for his magnificent oral elegy at the funeral of the first year's dead in the war against Sparta – though both speakers undoubtedly "smelled of the lamp" (as the common phrase put it, for burning the midnight oil in the preparation of a speech, however "extemporaneous" its presentation).

It is likely that the Sophists taught much of what would be offered in any good public-speaking course today: Keep eye contact with at least one member of the audience at all times; gesticulate sparingly but tellingly; liven up your style when the audience appears about to doze off or edge toward the door; be careful which hecklers you choose to answer and which you choose to ignore. And never talk down to your audience, ever – the orator who accurately gauges the intelligence and mood of the audience has won half the battle already. There is no more point in citing biblical chapter and verse to the heathen than there is in mentioning small dogs, good Republican cloth coats, or American apple pies in a plea to the justices of the Supreme Court, though as much has been tried. As far as speech-making is concerned, Protagoras was right: Man *is* the measure of all things, in particular, the man in the crowd in front of you, right now, listening to your speech, who will vote and act your way if he believes what you're saying and won't if you fail to convince him. (Naturally, all of the above applies equally to members of both sexes, not just males.) Despite the words of Socrates and Plato in favor of the Truth and against its obfuscation by clever argument, the legacy of the Sophists is still very much with us: Roosevelt was an effective public speaker, but then so was Hitler.

Before leaving the subject of rhetoric, we might add an etymological note: *Rhetoric* is related to the English "word" and its cognate "verb," the latter being derived from Latin. Although one might think otherwise (especially since the two words look alike and have quite similar meanings), *rhetoric* and *oratory* share no etymological connection. *Oratory* and the related form, *oracle*, come from the Latin verb meaning "to beseech, to pray." Latin *oratio* has the multiple sense of "language, prepared language, eloquence, style" and contrasts with *sermo* (whence English "sermon"), which means "plain, artless language."

Rhythm and *rhyme* (or *rime*, as it is often spelled) *are* related to each other, however. Greek *rhythmós*, probably related to the verb *rheîn*, "to flow," originally seems to have meant "a regular, recurring movement or motion, a measure." Thus, when we speak of the *rhythm* of speech or poetry, we are referring to its regular cadence. Greek poetry was unrhymed but metrical, the standard workaday meter of Greek being the dactylic hexameter, composed of six long-short-short feet, with the option of substituting a long for two shorts. When we speak of long and short syllables in English, there is some disagreement as to just what is meant by long and short, some holding that what we're really talking about is "stressed" versus "unstressed" while others maintain that the issue is really one of classical long and short vowels. In Greek there were no two ways about it: long vowels were long and short vowels were short (unless they were followed by a couple of consonants, in which case, they counted as long). The same held true in Latin, and the Romans cheerfully borrowed the Greek meters for their own use, relegating to the wastebasket their own native verse form, the Saturnian, of which so few lines remain that if anybody has ever figured out how it was supposed to work, it has remained a closely guarded secret. Eventually, the Latin language changed in such a way that the long-short distinction between vowels evanesced, and writing in the old borrowed Greek meters became an academic exercise.

For nonacademics, stress became the thing with an added fillip: *rhyme*, a descendant of the word *rhythmós*. As this word worked its way into the early Romance languages, it tended to be spelled phonetically, hence the English variant spelling, *rime*. It is possible that the native English word, spelled the same way and meaning "number," confused the issue, there being many a slip not only between cup and the lip but between lip and the pen, then as now.

Not that English speakers and writers have or have ever had a monopoly on slips of the lip or pen. Indeed, such slips have been known from time immemorial. *Rhotacism* – or, as U. Pani Shad et al. give it in their "Glossary of Linguistic Terminology," *rhotacirrm* – is one of the oldies but goodies, involving the substitution of *r* for some other sound, usually *s*. Examples abound in Latin, especially in nouns of the third declension whose nominative form ends in *s* and whose oblique-case forms show *r* in its place: *aes / aeris*, "bronze"; *genus / generis*, "type"; and older Latin *honos / honoris*, "honor," eventually replaced by the analogical form *honor / honoris*, presumably on the idea that if you can't lick – or pronounce – 'em, throw in the towel and call it a day.

◄ Σ ►

SIGMA

IS FOR *SYNTHESIS, SPHINX, SCYLLA,*
satyr, and *Symplegades.* A *synthesis* is, literally, "a putting-together; something which has been put together,"
the word itself being a putting-together of the Greek
preposition *sýn* and the noun *thésis.* *Thésis* comes from
the verb *tithénai,* "to put, place, set" and means "the
act or fact of putting, placing, setting." The Indo-
European root from which *tithénai* and *thésis* are derived seems to have been a very popular and well-worn
one; virtually all of the Indo-European languages, past
and present, preserve at least a trace of it, and most do
much better than that. Among the reflexes of this handy
root in English may be counted *do, deed, doom,* and the
-dom of *kingdom, serfdom,* and the like; *fact, facility,*
and the *-fy* of *nullify, rectify,* etc. (from Latin); and a
handful of useful Greek borrowings, such as *thesis,*
theme, apothecary, and *anathema.*

The origin of *sýn,* which means variously "with, together, same as," is tantalizingly obscure. Some would
like to derive *sýn,* with a little sleight of hand, from the
Proto-Indo-European root, **sem,* "one," which appears
plainly enough in such Latinate words as *similar, simple,*
simultaneous, and *singular,* and in such Sanskrit borrowings as *sandhi* and *Sanskrit* itself. (*Sanskrit,* the name of
the language spoken by the earliest Indo-European set-
tlers in India, literally means "unified, perfected (language)"; while *sandhi,* "a putting-together; a *synthesis,*"
is the grammatical term used to describe the process of
phonetic adjustment that takes place when words – or
parts of words – come together in running speech: "Jeet-
chet?" for "Did you eat yet?," "No, joo?" for "No, did
you?," "No, wanna?" for "No, want to?," and so on.

The double-barrel logic of the *sýn*-from-**sem* school of thought says that the things are both phonetically and semantically close. Unfortunately, this is largely controverted by the existence in Greek of plenty of other words that obviously go back to this same **sem* etymon but that have substantially different (and by no means problematic) phonetic outcomes in the language.

But, ah, a small knot of Indo-Europeanists at the back of the hall raise their hands and cry (in goose, alas) that there is an alternate form of *sýn* in Old Greek, *ksýn*, from which the initial *k* might have disappeared after saving the *s* from the ordinary fate of turning into *h*. True enough, though, unfortunately, the vowel still isn't right and the rest of the group is beginning to rattle its cutlery in anticipation of the frying of other more savory and substantial fish, so let us shrug our shoulders and move back onto firmer ground, consigning the origin of *sýn* to the warehouse of the world's linguistic mysteries, where it will have plenty of good company.

Let us say something certain about *synthesis*: It is by no means the only word in English with the prepositional prefix *syn-* in it, witness the existence of such indispensables as *synonym* (*sýn* in the sense of "same" and *ónyma*, the Aeolian form of regular Greek *ónoma*, "name") and *syntax* (*sýn* in the sense of "together" and *táxis*, "arrangement, ordering"). To these may be added the thinly disguised *sandhi* forms of *syn-* in *symphony* and *symbiosis*, *syllable* and *syllepsis*: Sounds go together in a symphony; different species live together in symbiosis to the common advantage of each, as when clover and its root bacteria fix nitrogen and enrich the soil, each allowing the other to live happily ever after; a syllable is the grasping-together of chunks of verbal sound; and syllepsis is the amalgamation of two basically different grammatical constructions pivoting on the use of a single word in more than one sense. Examples are: "Harry found a dollar in his pocket and that he had misplaced his luggage," in which "found" is doing double service.

Σσ

回回回

134

Compare "I took his advice and a taxi," or, "We stopped into O'Reilly's Tavern to bend our elbows and each other's ears." *Syllabub*, by the way, is not from *sýn* plus anything. This vile concoction of wine or beer mixed with milk or cream, which is then allowed to curdle and is served up whipped into a froth and sweetened with sugar comes from "silly" (i.e., "funny, happy") and "bub," which used to mean "strong liquor" and is of even more obscure origin than *sýn*.

Whatever else may be said about it, though, a syllabub *is* an imaginative synthesis of disparate elements, and as such constitutes a good stepping stone (on the rocks) to the grand subject of "figurative" synthetics, which will now occupy us.

For those who have not bolted for the door demanding their money back at the mention of "figurative synthetics," we mean no more than the imaginative putting-together of this and that, and offer the observation that the Greeks were great hands at it. (Putting things together in an imaginative way, as opposed to bolting for the door and demanding their money back, though here too they probably managed to hold their own if not someone else's.)

One of the more remarkable Greek syntheses was the *Sphinx*, a mythical being made up of the body of a lion onto which was grafted the head and breasts of a human female, as well as a pair of wings. (The so-called Sphinx of Egypt was the head of a particular king – Kephren – grafted onto the body of a lion and no real relation to the Greek monster at all, though the Greeks, on encountering the Egyptian "Sphinx" and seeing that it was a combination of lion and human being like their own, called it by the same name.) The Greek Sphinx was a fearsome creature, as suggested by its name, which comes from the verb *sphíngein*, "to throttle," (whence "sphincter," for what it's worth). The idea was that the Sphinx, of which a particularly ornery exemplar guarded the pass leading into Thebes, would throttle you if you didn't answer her riddle correctly. The riddle, in case you happen to encounter a Sphinx on your travels, was this: "What goes on four legs at dawn, two at noon, and three at nightfall?"

The equally legendary, though decidedly more anthropomorphic Oedipus, when asked the question, was able to come up with the right answer: "a person" (since in infancy, a person crawls on all fours, in later life walks on two legs, and in old age walks with a cane). The Sphinx, on hearing the correct answer, threw herself off the city wall and dashed herself to pieces, Rumplestiltskin style, and Oedipus went on to Thebes to marry the girl of his dreams.

Many have called Oedipus a monster for killing his father and bedding down with his mother, but it wasn't after all really his fault: *He* didn't know that Jocasta was his mother, and *he* didn't know that Laïos, whom he had slain for giving him too much lip in a traffic jam at rush hour on the road to Thebes, was his father. Oedipus had been raised in a foreign court with no knowledge of his real parents, after a shepherd had found him with his feet bound and badly swollen (*Oedipus* means "swollen-foot," the *-pus* part being the same as in "octopus" and "platypus" and akin to the *-pod* of "tripod"), having been left to die by his nearest and dearest rather than grow up to fulfill the dreadful prophecy of patricide and matrimony, which wound up coming to pass anyway in true dramatic fashion.

But ignorance was no excuse, at least as far as the Greeks were concerned: Apollo visited Thebes with a plague (though not until after Oedipus had married Jocasta, sired four children, and generally ruled wisely and well for a number of years), and this was all considered par for the course. For Sophocles, who wrote the most celebrated of the Oedipus plays, the moral of the whole business was, "Call no man happy until he's dead."

Many years later, though one can hardly say in a lighter vein, Sigmund Freud postulated that *all* little boys want to push their fathers out of the picture and enjoy their mothers' undivided attention and love, and so the "Oedipus Complex" was born. Subsequently, the notion that all little girls feel a corresponding desire to displace their mothers in their fathers' affections was put forth with comparable conviction and named with an equal eye to the classics. The "Electra Complex" gets its moniker from the story of Agamemnon's daughter Electra, who avenged her father's treacherous murder at the hands of her mother, Clytemnestra, after his long-awaited return from the Trojan War. We will not comment on these syntheses of classical tales and modern sexual stirrings, as that way lies madness, but it *is* worth noting that when Sophocles wrote the last of his Oedipus plays, *Oedipus at Colonus*, in which Oedipus appears as a wise and sympathetic old man, the author was ninety-two and in full possession of his faculties, writing the work in part as an object lesson for some of the younger members of his family who were trying to get appointed as his legal guardians on the grounds that he was too old and feeble to manage his own affairs.

So much for the Sphinx, may the Greek-she and the Egyptian-he rest in peace, and on to the *Scylla* (she who rends), another Greek synthetic female of prodigious and scarifying powers. Scylla was a six-headed monster who lived near the straits of Messina between the island of Sicily and the toe of the Italian land mass. She had long necks with dogs' heads on them, and she made a practice of eating people who came within easy reach. Odysseus and his crew were obliged to sail past her during the course of their wanderings, which would have been all well and good but for the fact that she worked in concert with another monster, the giant whirlpool Charybdis. (The two were the prototypical "if the left hand don't get you the right hand will" slap and tickle, and to this day "twixt Scylla and Charybdis" is a metaphor for a perilous middle route, or a choice between two equally dreadful evils.) Odysseus chose to skirt Charybdis by sailing close to Scylla, and lost six sailors while he was about it, but this was better than losing the whole ship down the drain and stopping the story in one fell swoop.

Then there were the *satyrs* – goat from the waist down, human from the waist up, if you discounted the horns on their foreheads. They were notorious for their lasciviousness, and *satyriasis* still persists as a medical term for pathological male horniness. (The female equivalent is *nymphomania*, since it was the nymphs that the satyrs were usually so anxious to debauch.) One satyr, Marsyas, was said to have picked up a flute that Athena had thrown away (because playing it distorted her features and injured her vanity). Marsyas became so proficient on the instrument, charming all he met (like the Indian god Krishna, whose flute-playing was said to charm the very milk from the bosoms of the ladies), that he got cocky and challenged Apollo to a musical duel. Apollo grimly agreed, and appointed the Muses as judges. They found in the god's favor and, as punishment, Marsyas was flayed alive.

Other synthetic creatures included centaurs – half horse, half human, and generally a nasty lot with the exception of Chiron, tutor to Aesculapius. Chiron was unfortunately struck by one of Herakles's poisoned arrows by mistake; although the gods had made him immortal he chose to die rather than live in perpetual torment, so asked that his immortality be given to Prometheus (who was doing time chained to a rock while a vulture came daily to nibble at his liver). This request was granted, and the gods, just to show they were good (if ironic) sports, put Chiron in the heavens as the constellation Sagittarius, the Archer. A more typical centaur was Nessus, who, when ferrying Herakles's wife Deianira across a river attempted to rape her. Herakles shot *him* with a poisoned arrow too, but Nessus had the last laugh: Affecting deathbed contrition, he told Deianira that if she steeped a shirt in his blood – a powerful aphrodisiac, he claimed – once Herakles put the shirt on, he would be faithful to her forever. As it turned out, centaurs' blood was a vitriolic poison, and as soon as Herakles put the shirt on, he was plunged into wild agony, so much so that he chose to burn himself to death on a pyre preferring, like Chiron, death to living in pain.

More synthetic monsters: the Chimera, a fire-breathing she-goat with a lion's head and a serpent's tail, slain by Bellerophon astride the winged horse Pegasus; a host of creatures noted for supernumerary parts: the Hekatoncheires or hundred-handed ones, sons of Kronos and Rhea, and who were the first blacksmiths; the Hydra, a polycephalic snake that grew two heads for every one you lopped off; the three-headed hellhound Cerberus, whom Herakles fetched up from Hades via Taenarum as one of his Twelve Labors; and Argus of the hundred eyes, guardian of the Golden Fleece, slain by Jason. Here too should perhaps be included the clashing rocks, or *Symplegades*, which guarded the entrance to the Bosporus. (*Symplegades* means something on the order of "the things that beat or weld together," the *sym-* part being our old friend *sýn* in mufti.) Jason and the Argonauts triggered the action of these rocks by sending a dove to fly through them first. When the rocks pulled back to reload, as it were, after nipping the dove's tail feathers, Jason's boat shot the rapids and got through without a scratch. In accordance with a previous prophecy, the rocks stayed put forever after and never ever gave anybody a hard time again.

T

TAU

IS FOR *TETRAHEDRON, TESSERACT,* AND
tesselation. All three of these geometrical wonders come
from the Greek word for "four," which in Ionic (eastern) Greek was *tésseres* and, in Doric (western) Greek,
téttares. This dialectal difference accounts for the variety
of forms English has borrowed from Greek (or, in the
case of *tessellation,* from Greek through Latin) with the
number "four" in them.

The *tetrahedron,* or four-sided pyramid, is the simplest
of the five "regular" solids, those geometrical figures in
three dimensions that may be constructed by joining
together planes of the same shape and size. The other
regular solids are the *hexahedron,* or cube; the *octahedron* (whose eight faces are all equilateral triangles); the
dodecahedron (whose twelve faces are all pentagons and
which is nowadays commonly seen as a desk calendar
with a different month of the year printed on each face);
and the *icosahedron* (whose twenty faces are, again, all
equilateral triangles).

The *tessarescaedecahedron* (from *tesseres / tettares-kai-
deka,* "fourteen"), by contrast, is the name given to one
class of the so-called "Archimedean" solids (since Archimedes was the first person to describe all thirteen of
them). These three-dimensional figures which, while not
regular in the strict sense in which the term is applied to
the "regular" solids, do have certain regularities to them.
The Archimedean solids are made from a mix-and-match
of regular plane figures – equilateral triangles, squares, and
hexagons – with no fewer than four of each type of face.
Two varieties of tessarescaedecahedron are the *truncated
cube* (whose corners are equilateral triangles) and the
truncated octahedron (whose corners are squares).

The *tesseract,* on the other hand, is a more recent invention, being a four-dimensional hypercube (from *tésseres,* "four" plus *aktís,* "ray"), though, since we can only visualize three dimensions at a time, *tesseract* commonly refers to the three-dimensional projection of what a four-dimensional cubic figure might be, much as we are wont to refer to the two-dimensional drawing of a cube as a *cube* with the attendant sleight of hand being forgiven (figure 1).

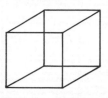

FIGURE 1

Tesseracts are generally represented in one or the other of two ways (figures 2 and 3), though in both cases, naturally, what we are talking about is a two-dimensional projection of a three-dimensional projection of a four-dimensional object, since the page is flat. In both cases, the integrity of the sides is sacrificed. In the projection in figure 3, all the edges are of equal length, thereby more graphically suggesting the idea of a three-dimensional solid traveling parallel to itself over a fourth dimension. Think of it as though the lower cube were a cube yesterday, the upper cube the same cube today, and the lines connecting the two its travel through the intervening night.

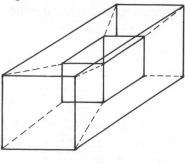
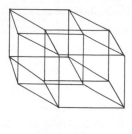

FIGURE 3

FIGURE 2

The reason why so many geometric terms in English come from Greek (including the word "geometry" itself, which literally means "measurement of the earth") is that the Greek mathematicians, with their peculiar blend of interests in the practical and the theoretical, were intensely concerned with the subject. They did not actually invent it – again, the Egyptians had gotten there first – but they did bring it to a high peak of refinement. (And as far as peaks are concerned, we should not forget to mention the *tessarace*, or, tetrahedral summit, from *tésseres/ téttares* plus *akē̆*, "point.") Undoubtedly the foremost, if not the first, among Greek geometers was Euclid of Alexandria, whose system of plane geometry was the standard among mathematicians and surveyors for millennia and whose teachings still persist in classrooms today. Indeed, non-Euclidean geometry (the geometry of curved space) is a fairly recent development that has only even more recently acquired real-world meaning with the discovery that massive objects, such as stars, bend light passing by them, making non-Euclidean space a reality. For everyday use, however, Euclid's geometry remains a thoroughly useful way of describing – and constructing – reality here on earth.

Euclid's life and times are known to us largely from baldly apocryphal anecdotes that date from some centuries after the fact. The principal source for what we *do* know is a commentary on Euclid's *Elements* by Proclus, who lived from 410 to 485 A.D., learned geometry at Alexandria, and later studied at Athens. Proclus dates Euclid as living at the time of Ptolemy I, the first Greek king of Egypt after Alexander the Great's conquest, which would put him around 300 B.C. Proclus says that Ptolemy came to Euclid asking if there might not be some easier way to learn geometry than by slogging through the *Elements*, to which Euclid was reported to have replied that, while in travel there were royal roads and roads for the common folk, in geometry there was but one road for all. (It is only fair to say that this same story, with a slightly different cast of characters, is also told about Alexander the Great and the geometer Menaechmus, but no matter.) Another story, appealing if of dubious authenticity, tells of a student of Euclid's who, after working his way through the "Definitions" that begin the *Elements*, asked, "But what shall I gain by learning all of these things?" Euclid is said to have summoned his slave and said to him, "Give this man three obols, since he has to be paid for everything he learns."

Much of what we know of Euclid's work we owe to the Arabs, who preserved his work in translation as they did the work of many other Greek authors lost in the original during the wanton destruction of the great libraries of antiquity as part of the spoilage of almost incessant war which plagued the Near East with its chronically uncomfortable aggregate of different peoples with different languages and world views. The first translation of the whole of the *Elements* into Arabic seems to have been done during the reign of the celebrated Harun-al-Rashid, caliph of Baghdad, who ruled from 786 to 809 A.D. The original Greek text forming the basis of the translation may have been the one removed from Byzantium some thirty years before in the wake of some unusually amicable dealings between the Greeks of that city and their Arab neighbors. (This occurred during the reign of the equally celebrated Caliph al-Mansur, slaughtered in the internecine squabbling that dogged the early days of Islam for, among other things, his blasphemous proclamation, *"Anu'l haq"* – "I am the truth".)

The first translator of the *Elements* into Arabic – one al-Hajjaj ibn Yusuf ibn Matar – was so successful under the Caliph Harun-al-Rashid that, on that Caliph's demise, he undertook a second translation (profusely illustrated) for the next Caliph, al-Ma'mun. Still later, another translation was produced by the son of the Christian physician to the Caliph al-Mutawakkil at some point before 910 A.D. This last served as the basis for the translation of the work into Hebrew some four hundred years later.

Baghdad, which served as the home of the Caliphs (one of the two lineages of Islamic leaders, the other being the competing Imams), was in its heyday a major cosmopolitan university town like Athens and Alexandria, drawing scholars from all over the "civilized" West. From Baghdad and the hinterlands came not only translations of the works of classical authors, Greek, Roman, and Indian, but a wealth of new vocabulary – "alcohol," "alembic," "alchemy," "Algebra," and "albatross," to mention only a few – and a wealth of ideas to go with them. One of these ideas was a wonderful fusion of geometry and art: the notion that you could tile a plane with decorated pieces of masonry of equal shape and size.

The art of tiling – *tessellation* – was highly refined by the Arabs, though the word for the art comes to us from Greek through Latin. In Latin, a *tessera* (from Greek *tésseres*, "four") was a cube, token, or ticket. A *tessella* was a small one. It is *tessella* that gives us our word "tile": A *tessellation*, then, is a pattern of cubes or tokens sunk into some sort of glue in such a way that the surface to be filled is completely covered with no unsightly protuberances when the job is done. Since most surfaces to be tiled were rectilinear – table tops, floors, walls, and the like, all of which are themselves most easily constructed with right angles – the simplest things to cover them with were also rectilinear, though it was soon discovered that triangles (two of which can make a square) and hexagons would also do in a pinch or in a flight of artistic inspiration. Far more complex patterns of repeating figures can be generated mathematically to tile a plane nowadays, as in the ingenious work of the late M. C. Escher, who, after seeing the Islamic tilings of the Alhambra in Spain, spent much of the rest of his life attempting to fill up all sorts of flat surfaces with interlocking devils and angels, black swans and white ones, fish and fowl, lizards and knights.

Tessellations were first made popular in the Greek world in the city of Byzantium, which held a peculiar position in the tug of war between the Old Greco-Roman civilization and the new Islamic society, which began its vigorous emergence with the rise to power of the prophet Muhammad in the early part of the seventh century A.D. While the followers of Islam were definitely down on many of the arts, the art of tiling, as long as it wasn't pictorial in the strictest sense of the term, was perfectly acceptable.

The Byzantines, not restricted to the depiction of inanimate figures (though they did experience a period of iconoclasm – the smashing of images – at a later point), refined the art of the mosaic to an unrivaled degree of perfection. ("Only Allah is truly perfect" would have been the Islamic comment of the day.)

The word "mosaic" comes from the Greek *mouseios* ("of or pertaining to the Muses," the multitalented daughters of the ever-randy Zeus and Mnemosyne, the personification of memory and, lest we forget, Zeus's aunt), whence also our word "music." (Oh, all right: The Muses were, in alphabetical order, Calliope, epic poetry; Clio, history; Erato, erotic poetry and mime; Euterpe, lyric poetry and music itself; Melpomene, tragic drama; Polyhymnia, holy prayer and singing; Terpsichore, song and choral dancing; Thalia, comedic drama; and Urania, astronomy.) The Byzantines were mostly Greeks, at least in the sense that they spoke Greek and considered themselves Greek at some level or another – though they had not gone untouched by the influence of their multilingual and multicultural neighbors to the east, just as they had not gone untouched by the influence of their Roman neighbors to the west. So the Byzantine fusion of Christian iconography with Islamic geometry was reasonable enough in Byzantium, however revolutionary it might have seemed to the rest of the known world.

This fusion found its expression in the Byzantine churches with their arched ceilings inlaid with *tessellae* or *tesserae* of different colors, depicting the Almighty, angels and archangels, and the saints, with the supernatural world extending by degrees downward to the congregation. Byzantine mosaic art conceived of the space in front of a picture and below it as an extension of the picture itself, a fact no straight-on photograph of a mosaic can recapture, since mosaics, when seen from below, seem to be foreshortened. (Images that only make sense when viewed from an unusual angle are called *anamorphic*, "formed again," because the image reforms itself aright only when one sees it from the proper angle or through a glass darkly.) The Byzantine mosaicists often set single figures against a background of gold-colored tesserae to make the figure seem slightly separated from the wall.

Byzantium itself remained a center for Greek and Roman culture long after the fall of Rome. The Roman emperor Constantine the Great had made Byzantium his capital in 330 A.D., and it managed to withstand both the assaults of the Germanic invaders to the north who eventually destroyed Rome and the pressure from the Arabs to the south. Although the city, renamed Constantinople, was sacked by crusaders in the thirteenth century and its extensive library was burned, it did not fall until 1453 A.D. when its walls were pounded by the first cannons at the hands of the Turks. At its height, the Byzantine empire stretched from Italy across mainland Greece and Anatolia (modern-day Turkey), and its cultural sphere of influence was even greater: It is to the Byzantine saints Cyril and Methodius that the Slavs are said to owe their Cyrillic alphabet. (According to one old saw, it resembles the Greek alphabet to the extent that it does only because the two missionaries were drunk at the time they endeavored to teach it to their northern neighbors, what with having over-fortified themselves against the cold.)

Lest we give the false impression that tessellations and mosaics were the *invention* of the Byzantines (with whatever help and inspiration from their neighbors to the southeast), though their refinement of the art is undisputed, we should mention at least one other group of practitioners of the art, the Romans. Roman mosaics were originally of two different types: *opus vermiculatum*, "worm-turning work" and *opus tessellatum*, "tessellated work." The chief difference between these two techniques of mosaic-making was the relative sizes of the tesserae used: *Vermiculatum* used very small tiles, enabling the artist to make fine, wavy lines, whereas *tessellatum* made use of larger, coarser building blocks. Sometimes *vermiculatum* would be the central picture and *tessellatum* the surrounding border. Eventually, the Romans abandoned the technique of *vermiculatum* as mosaics came increasingly to be used as permanent wall posters intended to be seen from some distance. Perhaps the most famous Roman mosaic of Magna Graecia is the picture of a baying hound with the inscription CAVE CANEM ("Beware of the dog") found in the floor of one of the grander houses unearthed at Pompeii, seventeen hundred years after the disastrous eruption of Mount Vesuvius in 79 A.D.

◄ Y ►

UPSILON

IS FOR *HYOID, HYPNOTISM, HYSTERIA,* *hydrant* and *Hydra, hypodermic, hyaline,* and *hubris.* All of these words begin with *h* in English because in Greek all initial *upsilons,* for some mysterious reason, were preceded by an *h* sound, or, "rough breathing." *Upsilon* (or, more properly, *ypsilon*) is an exception to this rule, the word being *y* plus *psilón,* that is, "bare, naked *y*."

The upper-case form of the letter gives us *y* with its various pronunciations. Speakers of Latin and the modern-day Romance languages pronounce the vowel represented by *y* as *ee,* distinguishing the letter from Roman *i* (from *iota*) – also used to represent the sound *ee* – by calling the former "*Greek i*" (or *i grec* in French and *i griega* in Spanish).

The lower-case form of the letter gives us Roman *u,* which in Latin was used to represent the sound *oo,* as it still does in all of the Romance languages except French. (By an accident of linguistic history, the pronunciation of the vowel in question is that known to the Greeks – a cross between an *ee* and an *oo* – an *ee* with concomitant lip rounding.)

The witty Sir John Harington, godson of Good Queen Bess, calls a privy "a shooting place writ with Pythagoras's letter," the Pythagoreans having thought that *upsilon* nicely symbolized the divergent paths of virtue and vice. Harington was speaking of toilet seats, whose connection with virtue or with vice may not be readily apparent, though one is reminded of the syphilitic's disclaimer: "Honest, Doc, I got it from a toilet seat."

In a somewhat more serious vein, there is the *hyoid* bone to consider. *Hyoid* comes from *hy,* the vowel sound itself, and *eîdos*, "form," the totality being the medical term for the U-shaped bone structure at the base of the tongue. Outside of medical terminology, which generally prefers the high – or highfalutin – Greco-Latin to the less expensive English spread, "Y-shaped" is the preferred designation of things shaped like an upper-case *upsilon*. For example, a divergent, bifurcating switch in railroad parlance is called a Y-switch (spelled "wye" by convention), and a forking intersection of roads is called a Y-square, at least in polite company.

Hypnotism (from Greek *hýpnos*, "sleep") is the placing of someone into a sleeplike trance. This process is otherwise known as "mesmerism" after its celebrated practitioner, Dr. Franz Mesmer (1735–1815 A.D.) who called it "animal magnetism." After enjoying great popularity as a parlor diversion, hypnotism was investigated as a psychiatric tool by Dr. Josef Breuer, who discovered that patients suffering from hysteria could recall under hypnosis the events that had triggered their condition, incidents too painful to be accessible to their conscious memory. Dr. Sigmund Freud then seized upon this revolutionary technique and began treating hysteria by the same method, publishing *Studies on Hysteria* jointly with Breuer in 1895, though he soon found that free association produced the same results and had a more long-lasting effect on the patient at that.

Hysteria, a psychosomatic condition with an incredible variety of symptoms, comes from the same root as the word *uterus*, *hýsteron* meaning originally simply "lower." Hysteria was formerly believed to be the result of disorders of the uterus, and was for many years a condition associated exclusively with women, much as dyslexia has been, until recently, a disorder associated exclusively with the male sex. (Recent research in both cases has tended to suggest that it has been the diagnostician, rather than the intrinsic nature of the malady, that has determined the sex-linking.) Many men, it has been suggested, while sharing the underlying psychopathology of "hysterical" women, have been diagnosed as simply compulsive or obsessive – when they have been diagnosed at all, since these traits are often seen as exemplary and good in the workaday world.

Hýsteron didn't only mean "lower," actually; it also meant "latter." This sense is revealed in the rather arcane term *hysteresis*, "the lagging behind of one of two related things," and in the marvelous double dactyl *hysteron proteron*, "the latter thing prior," a rhetorical figure involving the reversal of logical order, as when the departing performer of the last set at a jazz festival was announced by the master of ceremonies with the words, "He's gone; he's got his hat."

Two trochees beginning with the dactyl *upsilon* are *hydrant* and *Hydra*, both from Greek *hýdor/hýdatos*, "water," to which may be added the amphibrach *hydraulic* for good measure. A *hydrant* is a device which dispenses water, and if something is *hydraulic*, it works by means of water (or some other fluid) under pressure. (The word "hydraulic" comes from the Greek *hýdraulis*, the water organ invented by the Egyptian Ctesibius.) A *Hydra* was a sea serpent. *The* Hydra, whom Herakles slew (with a little help from his charioteer, Iolaus) as the second of his Twelve Labors, was a particularly fearsome sea serpent. Not only was her breath so bad that it could kill, she also had the ability to grow two heads for every one that got lopped off in battle. By the time Herakles arrived on the scene, she had nine heads. He managed to whack off eight of them, Iolaus promptly searing the necks to which they had been attached. The ninth head proved to be immortal, so Herakles buried it under a giant boulder and went on to his next labor, the catching of the wild boar of Erymanthus.

Under the microscope, a far less imposing sea creature was discovered in more recent times and given the name "hydra." This unassuming fellow has a stalk with a mouth at the top surrounded by tiny tentacles, and re-produces by growing new hydra now and again from a bud on the side of its central shaft. Nowadays, "Hydra" is used metaphorically for anything (usually bad) with a multitude of causes or which springs up afresh (with a vengeance) just as you think you've finally managed to stamp it out.

Another "water" word, *hygrós*, "wet," gives us easily as many useful words as the Hydra had heads, if not a few more to spare. Consider the *hygroscope*, which measures the humidity in the air, and *hygrometric* plants, which absorb and retain moisture (presumably against a nonrainy day). And what would life be like without *hygrostomia*, "salivation" or our *hygroblepharic* capabilities, which make possible the moistening of our eyelids and the generation of our tears?

By far the most productive class of *upsilon* words in English, however, is that which makes use of the Greek prepositions *hypó*, "under" and *hypér*, "over." A *hypodermic* syringe is designed to inject something under the skin (*dérma/dérmatos*). The *hypothalamus* is a little organ in the brain, located right under the thalamus. (*Thálamos* originally meant "inner chamber, storeroom, bedroom," the last sense of which is assumed in the old Greek masculine wheeze to the effect that a wife was at her best *thalámōi*, "in bed" and *thanátōi*, "dead.") And *hypothermia* (from *thermós*, "hot") is the medical term for when body heat drops – and stays – below what it ought to be. *Hypothermia* is what people who go out exploring in the cold often die of when their game plans hit a serious snag, and what sailors are advised to drown themselves rather than die of in case of shipwreck.

Hypertension, on the other hand, is high blood pressure or worrying too much, or both. The *hypercube* is a bit of high-powered (fourth-dimensional) mathematics. And *hyperemia* is an increased rate of blood flow to some part of the body or another, the *-emia* part being from Greek *haíma/haímatos*, "blood." *Hemophilia*, that scourge of the royal families of Europe, involves the unceasing flow of blood from even the smallest – let alone the unkindest – cut, and is a condition resulting from a congenital deficiency in the blood clotting factor, often the result of excessive inbreeding.

Beside the conventional fluid words – *hydro-* this and *hygro-* that, and the *hyper-* and *hypo-* "blood" terms that overrun the standard medical dictionaries – may be placed the Greek-derived words, like *hyaline*, "glassy," having to do with that singular fluid, glass, for which the Greek word was *hýelos*, an apparent borrowing (along with the technology of glass-making) from the Egyptians. Glass is essentially fused quartz sand with a few trace elements thrown in to lower the melting point. It has an amorphous structure and fractures conchoidally, unlike quartz crystals (whether grown deep in the earth when magma solidifies or in the laboratory under intense temperature and pressure), which fracture cleanly along the planes of crystallization. Molten glass is very flexible: A small blob can be blown into a large flask with thin walls, either in the air or into a mold. And hot glass can be easily sculpted with metal spatulas. However, stresses develop in glass as it cools, causing it to shatter catastrophically when struck or subjected to vast differences of temperature. This brittleness can be mollified somewhat by annealing – heating the glass object up again in a kiln until the stresses are redistributed and relieved – but the Greeks seem not to have known this, for Herodotus mentions that one of the wonders of the Persian court was a great glass drinking cup said to be shatterproof.

Tempered glass, a modern invention, goes annealed glass one better by exploiting glass's greater strength under compression (rather than under tension, which is why a glazier scratches one side of a pane of glass with a glass cutter and breaks it by bending the ends *away* from the scratch rather than *toward* it). To temper, a sheet of nearly molten glass is run between two cold rollers, which causes the surfaces of the pane to cool while the interior remains hot. When the inside cools it shrinks the already cooled surfaces, bringing them under compression. A school-laboratory version of this is the Prince Rupert drop, made by dropping molten glass into water: The surface cools immediately and the resulting teardrop cannot be broken by a hammer blow, but when the tail is broken off (and the compressional stresses relieved) the drop instantly shatters into tiny bits. Similarly, a sheet of tempered plate glass, when chipped, breaks into many tiny pieces – usually hexagonal – rather than big ones, as ordinary window glass does. Since glass is really still a fluid in its solidified state, window panes that have sat in their frames for fifty or a hundred years are noticeably thicker at the bottom, the glass having by infinitesimal degrees oozed its way downhill.

Although the Greeks used colored bits of glass in mosaics, it was the Romans who first exploited the decorative possibilities of glass in *objets d'art*. Archaeologists have found glass bars whose end section showed half of a human face; presumably two slabs were sawn off and mounted side to side for the complete picture. Glass as a window covering seems to have been a much later invention; the Latin word *panna*, "rag" (*pannae*, the plural, meant "swaddling clothes") gives us the *pane* in window pane, suggesting that speakers of Latin used other materials instead. The stained-glass windows of medieval cathedrals were strictly a public-works phenomenon, not within the budget even of the lesser nobility, let alone the common folk. Glazed windows in England were common enough by the eighteenth century so that a 1738 collection of graffiti bore the title *The Glass Window, or Bog-house Miscellany* (scurrilous verses were sometimes scratched on windows with a diamond, when not written on outhouse walls). Glass in the American colonies, however, was scarce, and large panes of it unheard of, hence the practice of filling a window frame with an array of much smaller diamond-shaped panes, latticed with lead – windows still preserved in the few remaining houses of the time.

Hubris is one of the only words in English where *upsilon* shows up as *u* instead of *y*. The word is often glossed as "tragic pride." Achilles's hurt pride cost the life of his boon companion Patroclus; Oedipus's resolute uncovering of the whole truth about his parentage cost the life of Jocasta and his own eyesight; and Julius Caesar's downfall and death was easily transformed by Shakespeare into a tale of a great man undone by his own pride. The Greeks felt that theatrical tragedy had to be played by the rules, in order that the audience not feel a shock to cosmic justice. Aristotle summed up some of them: All the action in a play had to take place in a single day and a single place; nothing violent could happen on stage, but had to be reported from off the scene or revealed (as when the chamber in which Agamemnon was slain is opened to the audience to reveal his dead body). And the tragic protagonist had to deserve his come-uppance even while exciting the sympathy of the audience to his humanity, which is where *hubris* comes in. A thoroughly virtuous man could not be brought down, nor a wicked one triumph.

These rules still make for good theater. The seventeenth-century French playwrights Racine and Corneille followed the rules to the letter – even the slap in *Le Cid* happens offstage and is reported, not seen. Today we have the ingenious adherence to classic rules in such popular works as the British novel *Billy Liar,* in which the likeable young picaro meets all his defeats in his home village inside of eighteen hours. Greek theory identified a particular flaw in character, called the *hamartia,* in each tragic figure: in Billy's case, untruthfulness; in Macbeth's, ambition; in Faust's, intellectual aridity; and in Don Giovanni's, lust. In all these cases *hubris* is the thematic disorder, though the particular *hamartia* of the protagonist makes for differences in plot. The moral of every great tragedy was, and is, "Pride goeth before a fall."

◄ Φ ►

PHI

IS FOR FANTASTIC PHENOMENA, BOTH
words being derived from the verb *phaínein*, "to bring to
light, make known, display" and its mediopassive coun-
terpart *phaínesthai*, "to appear, be brought to light,"
both ultimately from the noun *phôs* (originally *pháos*),
"light." Actually, *fantastic*, as well as *fantasy*, *phantasm*,
phantom (or *fantom*), and *phantasmagoria* (originally,
a magic-lantern display in which optical illusions were
produced for entertainment), come from the verb
phantázein, "to make visible," itself a reasonably transparent derivative of *phaneîn* through the addition of the
-z- infix signifying process (which appears in English as
-ize and *-ise*).

Other English spinoffs from the verb *phaneîn* having
to do with appearances, apparitions, and illumination
are:

diaphanous ("transparent, see-through"), used at
least 97 percent of the time as an epithet for women's
wear;

epiphany ("showing forth, revelation"), specifically
(and capitalized), the revelation of the infant Jesus to
the Magi;

phenocryst ("an easily visible crystal in an igneous
rock");

phenotype ("an individual that looks like another but
may be genetically different underneath it all");

phosphene ("an appearance of light" and, specifically,
"the appearance of rings of light when somebody pokes
you in the eye");

phase (as in "phase of the moon," that is, "the way
something appears at a given time");

emphasis ("special significance or prominence given to something");

hierophant (originally, "an explainer of the Eleusinian mysteries," that is, of the sacred rites of spring celebrated at Eleusis in honor of the goddess Demeter).

Hierós means "sacred, holy, supernatural," and the Eleusinian mysteries were all of that: Demeter was the goddess of grain; when her daughter Persephone was carried off to the underworld by Hades, Demeter refused to allow the earth to bring forth grain until Persephone was returned; after some heavy divine bargaining–Persephone had bound herself to Hades by inadvertently eating a pomegranate he had slyly offered her – it was decided that Persephone would spend the winter months of the year in the underworld and the rest of it back where she belonged, and the seasons could take their annual round, and the people of the earth could live happily ever after, celebrating the coming of spring in Eleusis. Now, with the advent of scientific farming, a *hierophant* is simply someone who explains something of obscure meaning. Another *-phant* (not "elephant," which comes from the Hamitic and Egyptian words for the beast and its ivory tusks) is worthy of mention: *sycophant*, "flatterer," whose first element comes from *sỳkon*, "fig." Thus, a sycophant was someone who made figs appear. The original meaning seems to have been "informer, accuser." What do figs, informers, and flatterers have to do with each other? Several etymologies have been suggested: (1) The reference is to fig-smuggling (illegal in ancient Greece), the idea being that the sycophant was the one who uncovered the telltale load of figs, for which act of civic helpfulness he might expect a reward. (2) The reference has to do with the shaking of a fig tree, thereby causing its fruits to leave their hiding place among the leaves and fall to the ground where all might see them, a metaphorical way of saying that the sycophant was someone who got rewarded for being an informer or bringer-to-light. Or (3) the reference was to "the sign of the fig," an age-old gesture (a fist with the thumb poking out between the index and middle fingers) signifying the female genitalia, the fig, like the pomegranate, being a standard symbol of fertility for its abundance of seeds. Apparently, the sign of the fig once functioned as quick and easy means of accusation of wrongdoing, similar in sense to thumbs down or the pointing of the accusatory index finger. The accuser, then as now, expected his reward; hence, the meaning now current of the term, as one who flatters in the hopes of a reward.

Phôs (genitive *phōtós*) itself yields a plentiful lexical harvest in English. The *photon* is a basic unit of light (formed by analogy to *proton, electron,* and *neutron,* the *-on* being the neuter nominative singular ending of first declension nouns in Greek). Ever since Newton, physicists had wanted to come up with a light particle that would do for illumination what the atom (from Greek *átomos,* "uncut, indivisible" from *témnein,* "to cut") had done for matter, that is, to reduce it to an ultimate level of indivisibility. (The earliest Greek version of atomic theory in general is attributed to Leucippus and his successor Democritus, who lived before and after the Persian Wars, respectively. Democritus is said to have been so astute that, on being first introduced to a friend's maidservant, he addressed her with "Good morning, maiden," but, encountering her on the following day, saluted her with "Good morning, madam," having correctly divined that she had been seduced in the intervening night. He is also reputed to have said, on another occasion, "I would rather discover a single cause than possess the kingdom of Persia," all very well to say for a person with an annual inheritance of a hundred talents a year from the Persian treasury. Democritus's father had been friendly with the Persian king Xerxes and had been granted a generous stipend, which Democritus spent on travel and study with the mathematicians and geometers of Egypt to everyone's general satisfaction and enlightenment.)

Photosynthesis, the basic mechanism of all plants' metabolism, is the putting-together of carbohydrates from carbon dioxide and water, using light as the source of energy (*sýn* "with, together" and *thésis*, "putting," from the verb *tithénai*, "to put, place").

A *photograph* is literally "light-writing," from *gráphein*, "to write" (originally, "to scratch, scrape"); and a *photoheliograph* is a device for taking pictures of the sun (*hélios* being the Greek word for "sun" – and metaphorically "light").

Appearances – how things looked in the light of day – were naturally very important to the ancient Greeks, and anyone else concerned with reality in those days. (*Evident* and *evidence* come from the Latin verb *vidēre*, "to see," cognate with the Sanskrit root *vid*, "to know," seeing and believing being from time immemorial inextricably bound. *Phenomena* were for the Greeks things that appeared, could be *seen*.) The difficulty, then as now, was that things are not always what they seem to be, hence our words *fantasy*, *fantastic*, *phantom*, and the like. (The reason, incidentally, for the double spelling of some words of Greek origin with *f* and *ph* is this: *Phi* originally represented an aspirated *p* sound, as in English "uphill" or "pickpocket," which eventually developed into an *f* sound in the ordinary course of linguistic history with its characteristic metamorphoses of sound, sense, and grammatical structure.)

The catalogue of Greek history and mythology is loaded with stories of mistaken identity, whether as a result of clever subterfuge or out-and-out physical change of form. (Both *identity* and *idea* come to us through Latin from Greek *ideîn*, "to see," from earlier Greek *wideîn*, cognate with Latin *vidēre*, "to see" and Sanskrit *vid*, "to know.") Theseus's father, for instance, threw himself off a cliff to drown in the sea on seeing the black sails hoisted on the ship that was to have brought his son home, signifying Minotaur – 1; Home Team – 0 in the latest bout between mortals and the beast. As it happened, it was all a ghastly mistake, for Theseus had triumphed and was alive and well; but unfortunately, the ship's crew inadvertently ran up the wrong set of sails. Other examples include Actaeon, who was changed into a stag as punishment for having peeped at Artemis in her bath; Daphne the water nymph, who became *daphné* the laurel tree in her eagerness to escape molestation by the randy Apollo; and Thetis who, seeking to escape similar advances by Peleus, changed herself by turns into fire, water, a lion, a snake, and a cuttlefish – all to no avail, which if nothing else, says something about Peleus's ardor and determination.

Or consider Odysseus, whose military cohorts were changed into swine by Circe, though they eventually recovered their human forms. Odysseus himself is credited for the greatest classical finesse in deception through the manipulation of normal appearances – social sand-throwing, if you will – to serve his own ends. The Trojan horse is ascribed to his fecund imagination. He is likewise said to have escaped from the clutches of the Cyclops by riding out of his cave grasping the underbelly of a giant sheep, fooling the blinded Polyphemus who only thought to check out the animal's woolly back to see if all was as it should be. Odysseus's return home disguised as a beggar is one of the high points of Western literature. The Greeks seem to have considered this sort of deception great stuff, acknowledging the disparity between appearance and actuality to be a legitimate source of good, clean fun. Their rather more stolid successors in the classical world, the Romans, were not so easily amused: By the time of Emperor Augustus, the poet Vergil could write of the great Greek hero with some scorn, contrasting Odysseus's craftiness with Aeneas's simple piety, manly courage, and unshakable doggedness. But then, when the Romans wanted someone with just the right mixture of ingenuity and insight, they tended to hire a Greek for the job.

It is not surprising, in a world in which "seem" and "be" were often not one and the same, that there should be such a thing as fear. While the Greeks did not of course invent fear, they did coin the word *phobia*. After centuries of use by both Greeks and Romans alike, this term has come down to us in pristine condition. A look at the lexicon of English reveals some three hundred established words ending in *-phobia*, designating a somewhat smaller number of morbid fears or dread aversions, some so fundamental that there is more than one word each for them (e.g., *gatophobia, aelurophobia,* and *galeophobia,* all referring to a pathological dread of cats).

As a set, the phobias named in English constitute an interesting gloss on the culture and our construction of reality, past and present. Some of these come to us directly from Greek, old tried and true fears, such as *triskaidekaphobia* (fear of the number thirteen); *cypridophobia* (fear of Aphrodite who was sometimes called Cypros because she was said to have washed ashore on the half shell at Cyprus – therefore, fear of sexual intercourse or of contracting venereal disease); and *acousticophobia* (fear of strange noises or things that go *bump* in the night). Other fears come to us from the Romans through such Latin and Greek hybrids as *claustrophobia* (fear of being enclosed, from Latin *claustrum,* "enclosed space," whence English *cloisters*); *sinistrophobia* (fear of things on one's left side, from *sinister,* "left"). This last fear was common enough, apparently, among speakers of Latin that the need was felt to create another word, *levophobia,* with almost the same meaning. *Noctiphobia* is poetically defined by *Dorland's Illustrated Medical Dictionary* as "morbid dread of night and its darkness and silence." Other fears smack of more recent invention: beside the traditional *xenophobia* (fear of strangers, foreigners), we find *Francophobia* and *Gallophobia* (fear of the French), *Germanophobia* and *Teutonophobia* (fear of the Germans), *Japanophobia* (fear of the Japanese), and, of course, *Russophobia* (fear of the Russians). Oddly enough, though, while there seem to be named fears for virtually everything in the known universe (including "everything," for which there is a plurality of terms), nobody seems to have thought to coin a term for fear of the unknown. This is left, as they say, as an exercise for the student.

◄ X ►

CHI

IS FOR *CHASM*, *CHAOS*, AND *CHRIST*.
Both *chasm* and *chaos* come from the verb *chaínein*, "to
yawn, gape," a *chasm* being a yawning abyss, and *Chaos*
being *the* original yawning abyss from which, according
to the early Greeks, everything and everyone ultimately
made their leap into the universe of discourse, ascending
from the disorder and confusion of the great unknown
into the ordered cosmos that we all know and love.
Christós, "Christ, the Anointed One," comes from the
verb *chríein*, "to anoint."

The Greeks were good candidates for Christianity,
with its particular ordering of the world and the here-
after, thanks to the strong streak of humanism running
through their culture for the preceding five centuries.
Indeed, the Christians' heaven and hell owed much to
preexisting Greek ideas about the afterlife. Moreover,
the Greeks already had the concept of a "savior" in their
spiritual vocabulary: *Sōtér*, "Savior," was an epithet of
the highest of their native gods, Zeus. In addition, the
Greek words *Iésous Christòs Theoû* (*H*)*Yiòs Sōtér*
("Jesus, the Anointed, the Son of God, the Savior")
formed the convenient acronym *ichthýs*, "fish," which
tied in very nicely with the fish imagery so closely associated with the early Christian movement: fish as a familiar
ancient Near Eastern symbol of fertility and life; fish as
the natural stock in trade of the residents of the region
surrounding the Lake Gennesaret (and the Mediterranean) and the local staff of life; fish as metaphor (the first
followers of Christ were exhorted to be "fishers of men");
and, possibly, fish as a quick and easy thing to scrawl on a
wall to keep the faith in the public eye in a time of
official hostility, much like the modern peace sign or

the Omega, signifying resistance to military conscription.

And, to top it all off, the Athenians had an altar previously dedicated to "the Unknown God," which Saint Paul lost no time in announcing was none other than the Christians' God, and, in advancing cogent arguments to that effect, won over many Greeks on first hearing. (Despite his extraordinary energy and oratorical power, the Apostle was not so successful at Ephesus in Asia Minor, where his advance man was shouted down by the crowd who had gathered to hear him out, crying "Diana of Ephesus is great!" Local pride, it is only fair to say, may have played a part here: The temple of Diana at Ephesus is generally reckoned one of the seven wonders of the ancient world.)

The advent of Christianity heralded a profound change in the way people would look at the world for ever after, whether they accepted or rejected the faith. The fact that Christianity was born into a world that could be reached by the power of the written word was not lost on the early exponents of the faith. (And it is interesting to note that the Angel Gabriel is quoted as saying, in his first revelation to the prophet Muhammad some six hundred years after the birth of Christ, "Your Lord – Allah – is the Most Bounteous One, Who by the pen has taught mankind things they did not know.") Christianity owes a great deal to the alphabet for its success among the world's people, a debt which it has more than amply repaid, first and foremost by offering the illiterate an incentive – the Scriptures – to become literate, and, second, by imbuing the letter X – chi – with a wealth of meaning that it would undoubtedly not have had otherwise. Consider the following uses of X as symbol:

X stands for Christ, as in Xmas, partly as a sign of the cross and partly as the first letter of His name. Another code sign for the name of Christ is ☧ (chi-rho), the first two letters of His name in Greek. (This is apparently

unrelated, folk etymology notwithstanding, to the prescription sign ℞ , for Latin *recipe*, "take," which may be
akin to the astrological sign ♃ for Jupiter or, more
likely, may be a fancy abbreviation for *praescriptio*,
"prescription.") Curiously, X for Christ has in some
cases been conspicuous by its absence: The Irish Celts
avoided the use of the Roman numeral X in writing because they associated it with Christ's name; and the
Chinese, after some contact with the West, deleted all
cross motifs from their coinage for much the same reason, though for them the connotation was thoroughly
negative.

X stands for the crucifix or cross, both Christ's and, in
medieval times, that of Saint Andrew. Thus, a sign reading PED XING is nowadays used to mean "pedestrian(s)
crossing." Similarly, some gestures involve a cross or
crossing, as in "Cross your heart (and hope to die)" and
"I'll keep my fingers crossed," the first being an exhorta-
tion to tell the truth (or else), and the second, a prayer
for good luck. Crossing your fingers has a double meaning: If you cross your fingers out of sight of the hearer
while telling a lie, you are somehow absolved from the
usual punishments for distorting the truth. Crossing your
arms on your chest to reassure a hostile dog that you
mean him no harm (and that he should therefore not
give you a hard time) may have a similar origin; likewise,
the perfidious double-cross. Other Xs with a double edge
include the X of the Runic alphabet of the Vikings – the
Hargale – which stood for bad luck, and the more modern
crossed matchsticks, which stand for *good* luck. The X
of the skull and crossbones of pirates and poison, and
the X for a wrong answer all bode no good, but probably
all owe their origin to the power of the Christian cross.
All are in some sense warnings.

X is for a kiss, which may derive from X for Christ as
love or from the sound of the letter as it appears in our
Roman-derived alphabet, which used X to represent *ks*,
rather than the aspirated *k* sound for which *chi* was

used in the alphabetic writing of the eastern Greeks. Hard to say.

X is a marker of proof. Both tinsmiths and brewers of strong drink used a system of single, double, or triple Xs to advise the consumer as to the consistency of the alloy and the potency of their beverage. X as a designation of the strength of the maker's product seems to have carried over to the manufacture of high explosives, and at least one brand of male contraceptive, in more modern times.

X has also stood for the signature of the illiterate: "X So-and-So, his mark" is well attested, the "So-and-So, his mark" being written by a literate witness.

X also marks the spot: To establish a point, draw two lines through it, since any point can be defined as the intersection of two lines (or line segments). Carpenters have tended to abbreviate this marking to V to avoid confusion with X as an expression of "cross it out and remeasure it." X, in free variation with the check mark, is still used to mark the ballot or the multiple-choice answer on many other standardized tests.

X and Y chromosomes get their names from their characteristic alphabetic shape. The so-called "wild type" has the normal number of X and Y chromosomes, while the "criminal type" has an extra X (XXY instead of the ordinary male "wild type" XY), "wild" in this case meaning "occurring naturally." In the world of domestic cats, known from the time of the Egyptians, an extra X chromosome is the culprit in the case of male calico (black and orange) cats: Toms with the ordinary number of X and Y chromosomes are either orange or black but not both at the same time.

X also stands for the syllable *eks*, as in *X*tra for "extra" and *X*ec for "exec(utive)." Here the western Greeks and the Romans have been at work with the language.

In algebraic notation, X stands for a good baker's dozen of things. (For a complete rundown, the reader is encouraged to have a look at Florian Cajori's *A History of Mathematical Notation*.) × as a sign for multiplication – a relatively recent concept in the history of mathematics – first makes its appearance in English in the great Oughtred's *Clavis Mathematicae* (*The Key to Mathematics*), published in 1631. A controversy has been roiling for centuries as to the ultimate source of this sign, some holding that it makes reference to the Venetian system of "multiplying by the cross," a system sufficiently abstruse to excuse us from the onus of attempting to explain it here. (Cajori offers eleven other possibilities in the space of a paragraph.) The other standard sign for multiplication – the raised dot – was suggested by the philosopher Leibnitz.

Perhaps more interesting is the use of X as an algebraic unknown, not that its origin is any less obscure than that of X for multiplication. Diophantus was the first Greek mathematician to introduce the alphabetical unknown into algebraic problem solving.. (The word *algebra* itself comes to us from the medieval Arabs, *al jebr* meaning "the putting together" of something with something else.) Diophantus flourished in Egypt at Alexandria in the middle of the third century of the Christian era, three hundred years or so before the Arabian hegemony. X as the unknown is still popular – Brand X, X rays, Planet X, X the anonymous author, and the X adopted as the surname of members of the Black Muslim movement – all of these are ongoing uses of this versatile letter of the alphabet.

One more use of the letter X should be mentioned: that of X as numeral. The Greeks used X (the letter *chi*) for 600 in their alphabetic system of numbering in which each letter of the alphabet – including three that had previously been dropped: *digamma, koppa,* and *sampi* – was assigned a numerical value. By writing letters next to each other, it was possible to represent the quantities for which there was no single-letter symbol. Somewhat confusingly, X (*chi*, the first letter of the word *chílioi,* "1000") was also used to stand for 1000. A third seminumerical use of X in Greek was as an abbreviation

Xχ

for *chalkoûs*, the Greek farthing, valued at one-eighth an obol, which was derived from *chalkós*, "copper." The use of X as the Roman numeral for ten is obscure in origin, though some interesting possibilities have been suggested: (1) that it derives from the use of tally sticks, either as two crossed sticks to designate "ten," or from the crossing out of ten vertical lines, similar to the way that we mark a tally of five by drawing a diagonal line through four vertical lines; (2) that its origin is from the Roman numeral V for five: an upside down V attached to a rightside-up V, the V being derived either from the schematic representation of a hand with the four fingers sticking out one way and the thumb another, or from tally sticks (or from half an X); or (3) that it represents a schematic rendering of crossed arms, i.e., crossed hands, each with its five fingers.

◄ Ψ ►

P S I

IS FOR *PSYCHE, PSALTERY, PSALMS,* AND
pseudonym. Psyché comes from the verb *psychein,* "to
breathe" (probably of onomatopoeic origin) and originally meant "breath, life, spirit, soul." The personification of *Psychē* was natural enough: She was, according
to legend, the beautiful daughter of a king, so beautiful,
in fact, that her very existence infuriated Aphrodite, the
goddess of love, to such a degree that she resolved to
make Psyche fall in love with the ugliest man possible.
To accomplish this unfriendly end, Aphrodite sent her
son Eros (Roman Cupid) to take care of the details. Unfortunately, Eros fell in love with the princess himself
and carried her off to a palace where he visited her only
by night, warning her not to try to see what he looked
like.

Apprehensive that she had in fact wound up with the
ugliest man possible or – far worse – some gentle monster,
Psyche one night lit a lamp and looked on Eros's face
while he slept. A drop of hot oil dripped from the lamp
onto Eros's shoulder and he awoke. After roundly scold-
ing her, Eros departed, whereupon Psyche set out to
find him, traveling widely without success until she came
to the temple of Aphrodite. There she was told to per-
form a series of impossible tasks, which, like most fairy-
tale royalty in love, she somehow managed to accomplish, albeit with the aid of Eros himself while nobody
was looking. Aphrodite, impressed and somewhat mollified, allowed Psyche to marry Eros, making her immortal
into the bargain. They are presumed to have lived happily ever after, their daughter in the Latin version of the
story being named Voluptas ("sexual pleasure").

Psyche in English generally has the sense of "mind" or

"spirit," two words with traditionally overlapping meanings. ("Mind" comes from an Indo-European root meaning "to think, remember" and "spirit" comes from the Latin word *spiritus*, which originally meant "air, breeze, breath" and later took on the meaning of "breath of life, life, disposition, energy.") By and large, in this scientific day and age, "mind" without any hocus-pocus is what *psyche* means, as in the following compounds: *psychology* ("study of the mind"), *psychoanalysis* (a means of investigating a person's mental processes with an eye to fixing them when they've gone awry), and *psychotherapy* (a rather more nuts-and-bolts approach to the treatment of mental or emotional disorders, generally less expensive and less time-consuming than psychoanalysis).

The *o* in *psychology, psychoanalysis,* and *psychotherapy,* in case you were wondering, is spurious. (If you weren't wondering, never mind.) It shows up in these words by analogy to all sorts of *-ology* words, like *astrology* and *anthropology,* in which its occurrence is perfectly kosher because the *o* is part of the noun stem to which the suffix *-logy* has been added. Note that in German, "psychoanalysis" shows up as *Psychenanalyse,* and in British English it's *psychetherapy,* not "psychotherapy."

Other *psyche* words worth mentioning are *psychotic* (i.e., severely disturbed) and *psychosis,* which, like the milder *neurosis,* is built on the model provided by all sorts of other *-osis* words generally naming degenerative diseases of that part of the body signified by the combining root: *retinosis,* "a degenerative condition of the retina"; *hepatosis,* "a disorder of the liver"; and so on. *Psychic* can mean simply "of or pertaining to the mind," though *psychological* is the preferred word for this sense so that *psychic* may be reserved for use in describing phenomena or perceptions attributed to the power of mind over matter. "Psychic phenomena," sometimes known as "parapsychological phenomena," are things that *seem* to happen, things that people think they have experienced, but which cannot be explained by the ordinary "laws" of science and the physical world – extrasensory perception, mental telepathy, and the like. "Psychic energy" is what most people feel drained of at the end of a nine-to-five, five-day week when Friday afternoon rolls around. Many, though, have been known to experience this mysterious loss of power as early in the week as first thing Monday morning, possibly because they don't have enough music in their lives, against which eventuality the *psaltery* was invented.

A *psaltery*, for those who have never suffered from Sunday night insomnia or the Monday morning blahs, is a stringed instrument akin to the dulcimer and zither, whose pleasant sound is produced by plucking the strings. (*Psaltery* comes from the verb *psállein*, "to twang.") History has not recorded the names of the first people who realized you could make music by stretching a string or strings across a frame (or, later, a frame with a resonating chamber behind it), but the earliest Greek to undertake a systematic investigation of the acoustical properties of strings was undoubtedly Pythagoras, who flourished in the sixth century B.C.

According to various reports, some of which are probably reliable, Pythagoras was born on the island of Samos during the reign of the tyrant Polycrates. From there, either because the political climate became too warm or simply because he wished to satisfy his wanderlust and prodigious curiosity, Pythagoras set out for the neighboring island of Miletus, where he is said to have studied with the great scientist, Thales, later moving on to Phoenicia and Egypt and, later still, to Babylon. He eventually returned to Samos where he founded a mystical-mathematical order whose members also dabbled in politics, resulting in their hasty departure for the city of Crotona in Magna Graecia.

Among their various scientific endeavors was the systematic study of the harmonic relationships in what might be called acoustical space. Pythagoras, or the Pythagoreans, discovered that the harmonic intervals of the diatonic scale could be generated by stopping a fixed string of given length at various points: halfway for the octave, a third of the way for a fifth, a quarter of the way for a fourth, and so on. The shorter you make the string, the faster it will vibrate when you pluck it and the higher the tone that you'll get. In wind instruments, which the Pythagoreans did not investigate, the process is much the same. In a flute, for example, you produce the octave essentially by overblowing, that is by blowing harder: The greater force causes the column of air inside the instrument to vibrate twice as fast, which it why it's hard to play a flute loudly in its lowest octave *without* overblowing, as any beginning flute player will readily attest.

The Pythagorean discovery of the relation of string length to musical tone was one of many useful pieces of information that came out of their research into the mathematical ratios, which they hypothesized underlay the workings of the natural world. Another such was the discovery that a triangle inscribed in a semicircle (with one side being the diameter of the circle) is always right-angled. Perhaps the most famous fruit of the Pythagoreans' researches was the revelation that the square on the long side of a right triangle (the hypotenuse) is equal to the sum of the squares on the other two sides, that is, if you draw a square with the hypotenuse of a right triangle as its base, this square will be equal in area to the combined areas of the squares drawn in like fashion, with the other two legs of the triangle as their bases.

This latter discovery is called the Pythagorean Theorem or Pythagorean Relation, and provides the basis for the following shaggy dog story: A Cherokee chief had three wives. He installed each in a separate domicile and provided each with a carpet made from the hide of a different animal: One was given a deer-hide carpet, another was given a bear-hide carpet, and the other was given – however implausibly – a hippopotamus-hide carpet. In time, the wife who had been given the deer hide became pregnant, and the chief asked the local soothsayer for a prognosis, to which the soothsayer replied that the happy couple could expect a healthy son. And so it came to pass. The wife who had been given the bear hide then became pregnant and the soothsayer predicted, rightly, a healthy daughter. When the third wife, the one who had been given the hippopotamus hide, became pregnant, the soothsayer predicted twins, again rightly. The chief, marveling at the soothsayer's powers of prediction, asked, "How could you tell that it would be *twins?*" to which the soothsayer replied, "A simple calculation, really, since, as we all know the squaw on the hippopotamus is equal to the sum of the squaws on the other two hides."

It is quite possible that the theorem involving the inscription of a right triangle in a semicircle was discovered by observation (while the other must have taken quite a bit of thinking), since the standard Greek method of drawing a circle in the first place was to fix a string at the center of the would-be circle and drag the other end around, holding it taut. To draw an *ellipse*, one fixes *two* points and guides the string in a loop, the two points being called the *foci* (Latin *focus*, "hearth," or center of the household, and the word from which most of the modern Romance languages have derived their word for "fire"). *Foci*, the plural of *focus*, was aptly appropriated by the seventeenth-century astronomer Johannes Kepler in his demonstration that the orbits of the planets are not circular, as had previously been supposed, but elliptical, with the sun one focus of the ellipse. (This discovery made possible another shaggy dog story the enterprising reader may reconstruct from its punch line: "The boys called their beef ranch 'Focus' because that's where the sons raise meat [sun's rays meet].") Kepler, it might be added, shared Pythagoras's harmonic mysticism and spent the latter part of his life expounding a rather spaced-out astronomy in which the ratios of the sizes of the planetary orbits were held to recapitulate actual harmonic ones, thus producing the "Music of the Spheres."

The Pythagorean Order, like most early Greek religious societies, exacted a set code of behavior from its initiates, who were classified into two ranks: the *akousmatikoí*, or "auditors," and the *mathēmatikoí*, or "esoteric students." They all rose early in the morning and set to recalling in minute detail everything that had passed the previous day, abstained from certain foods, exercised in gymnastics and music, and were expressly enjoined not to noise around any of the Order's secret teachings. One of these – that the square root of two could not be represented as a whole-number fraction – gave the group such anxiety, disruptive as the notion was of the Pythagorean view of a cosmos reducible to tidy whole numbers, that "auditors" were not permitted to hear about it.

Eventually, the solidarity of the Order got everybody into trouble in Crotona whither, as mentioned earlier, Pythagoras had moved his ashram in the wake of similar difficulties in his native Samos. The upshot was that the aging philosopher was murdered in a particularly vehement conflict between town and gown during the time of Tarquin the Proud, the last Etruscan king of Rome. Offshoot Pythagorean fellowships then established themselves in other cities of Magna Graecia, notably at Sybaris (where these politically active esthetes must have had a rather cool reception, as *sybaritic* still endures as a term for Corinthian-style luxury and debauchery), Metapontum, and Tarentum, where their reception was not much better.

So as not to leave the subject of the psaltery and the harmony of the spheres on so sour a note, let us quickly mention *psalms*, those songs meant to be sung to the accompaniment of a stringed instrument. We are told that David used to play the harp (a psaltery without the refinement of a resonating chamber) to soothe King Saul during the latter's periodic psychotic episodes. *Psalm*, like psaltery (and *psalter*, "a collection of psalms"), comes from the verb *psállein*. The derivation of English "feel" and "palpate" from the same source may or may not be a case of pseudoetymology.

Pseudo- (from Greek *pseûdos*, "false") means "fake," of course, and is a highly productive prefix in English: Any phonus balonus can be put in his or her place by the simple addition of *pseudo-* to the person's profession or pretension, as in *pseudointellectual, pseudoscientist,* and *pseudosanitation engineer* (a person masquerading as a garbage collector). Some *pseudo-* words are well-established as a part of the language, as, for example, *pseudonym,* a fake name usually adopted by authors who wish to avoid literal or legal brickbats, unwanted invasions of privacy, or excessive amounts of junk mail. Actors and actresses often ply their trade pseudonymously, though generally for the sake of greater euphony or acceptability by a wider audience. These pseudonyms are generally referred to as "stage names."

Some famous pseudonyms: Lewis Carroll whose real name was Charles Lutwidge Dodgson; the actors Danny Kaye and Mel Brooks, both of whom were born with the surname Kaminski; Peter Warlock, the composer, whose given name was Philip Arnold Heseltine; the authors George Eliot (née Marian Evans) and George Sand (Amantine Aurore Lucile Dupin, Baroness Dudevant); and the Bell "brothers," Currer, Acton, and Ellis (Charlotte, Anne, and Emily Brontë, respectively), who, like the two "Georges" just mentioned, published under masculine-looking pseudonyms because they knew damn well their work would be taken much more seriously if it looked as though it had been written by a man. And indeed, the "Bell" book was well-received until the secret crept out, at which point, sales plummeted. Similarly, Louisa May Alcott published some lurid tales under the pseudonym of A. M. Barnard knowing full well that her male readers would not only be titillated but downright horrified to think that a woman might have written this stuff.

Other *-nyms,* while we are on the subject, are every

bit as pervasive in English as those of the *pseudo-* variety, and so merit at least passing comment. *Eponyms* are regular everyday words, like mesmerize, maverick, silhouette, boycott, and braille, that owe their existence to real people: Franz Mesmer, Samuel Maverick, Étienne de Silhouette, Captain Charles Boycott, and Louis Braille. Begonias, forsythia, gardenias, and poinsettia all take their names from real people (Michel Bégon, William Forsyth, Alexander Garden – his real name – and Joel Poinsett) as do the diesel engine and the Pullman car.

There *should* be such a thing as a *paronym* – from *paronomasia*, "punning" from the verb *paronomázein*, "to use one name in place of another" – but, alas, the word *pun* (from Latin *punctus*, "point") has already been adopted in its place. We still have *homonyms*, though, words that sound the same but have different referents. Sometimes the spelling will disambiguate the ambiguity: *sun* and *son*, *meet* and *meat*, *rays* and *raise*, and the like. At other times, more drastic measures are required. Lord Russell, the conservative, was once written a letter by the liberal Bertrand Russell after the latter's succession to his late brother's title. Bertrand suggested that the two of them publish a letter in the *London Times* avowing that each was not the other – a typical bit of philosophical mischief on Lord Bertrand's part. Or consider the case of one John Toilet who went to court to petition for a change of name. The presiding magistrate asked, "Well, what is your name?" to which the humble petitioner replied, "John Toilet." Hearing him say so, the magistrate remarked, "Well, I shouldn't wonder that you'd like to change your name. To what would you like to change it?" To which the man replied, "*Martin* Toilet." "*Martin* Toilet?" "Yes. You see, there's a fellow who lives down the street with the same name as mine and I keep getting all his mail."

OMEGA

IS FOR *OCEAN*. THE EARLY WORLD OF
the Greeks was little more than the Mediterranean Sea
and the lands along its coast. Common belief had it that
beyond these known regions lay a giant circumferential
river, called *Ōkeanós* (whence English *ocean*), which
was sometimes personified as *Ōkeanós*, the son of
Ouranos (the sky) and Gaia (the earth). Even so great
a light as Eratosthenes, who firmly believed that the
earth was a sphere capable of being measured, shared the
opinion of his contemporaries that the whole business
was surrounded by ocean. For the most part, the straits
of Gibraltar, known as the Pillars of Herakles, were as
far west as most Greeks dared to venture, leaving the
exploration of the vast beyond to their adventurous
neighbors, the Phoenicians, from their home ports of
Tyre and Carthage.

The Phoenicians, like the Vikings a millennium later,
were bold seafarers who traded and raided along the
coasts, establishing colonies wherever they went. (The
Greeks of Homer's time did this too, though by and
large they confined their activities to the Aegean.) In
the fifth century B.C., Hanno, the governor of Carthagin-
ian Spain, sent an expedition out past Gibraltar and
down the coast of Africa as far as Sierra Leone. Eventually, the Phoenicians are said to have circumnavigated
the whole of Africa, a feat not to be repeated, as far as
anyone can tell, until the Renaissance.

Likewise exploring northward, the Phoenicians established tin mines in Cornwall and brought back amber
from the coast of Frisia, tin and amber being commodities that fetched a pretty price indeed in the Mediterranean. Some time in the middle of the fourth century

B.C., one Pytheas set out from his native (Greek) city of Massilia (modern-day Marseilles) on a long and ambitious voyage, skirting the coast all the way to the British Isles and the North Sea beyond. He is credited with the discovery of a place called Thule (*Thoúlē*) some seven days' sail from Britain. Unfortunately, the records Pytheas kept of his trip have come down to us in fragmentary form, so no one to this day knows for sure just where Thule was supposed to be, though a good guess is probably Iceland. For a thousand years, Thule – the "Ultima Thule" of Seneca's verses and many fanciful (and not so fanciful) maps of the world by a variety of early cartographers – remained the farthest flung "known" land to dwellers of Europe and the Near East. Two centuries after Pytheas's expedition, the Romans came to power, smashing the naval forces of the Phoenicians, thereby curtailing any serious exploration of the world's waters for some time to come.

For the Greeks, stories of the sea made up a great part of their literary stock in trade, running the gamut of genres from high art to the local equivalent of science fiction: After all, once you got beyond the Pillars of Herakles, well, *anything* might be out there. Some opined that this "outer space" terminated abruptly, and even the greatest ship might tumble over the edge like a man in a barrel going over Niagara Falls. Even those who thought that the earth might well be spherical were known to hold the view that the surrounding Ocean, once you got into it, might prove to be thick, like mud, or might be ringed by an area of perpetual darkness, the latter notion being a reasonable enough extrapolation from reports of real experience in the exploration of the far northern waters in winter. And for their part, the Phoenicians, being coast-huggers, couldn't have contributed much to dispel these flights of Grecian fancy, for they never strayed out into the open Atlantic unless blown off course, which did of course happen from time to time and probably resulted in the discovery and loss of the Canary Islands many times over. Indeed, the Canaries may well have provided the original for the Thule-like "Fortunate Isles" that appear in early maps and sea lore but which modern people have never been able to pinpoint exactly. The Fortunate Isles were said to be the home of the Hesperides – "daughters of the evening" – whose mother was Hesperis, the Evening Star, and who fulfilled the useful function of guarding the golden apples that Hera was given on her wedding to Zeus. (Whether any other wedding presents of dubious utility were stored in this faraway place is not clear, though the idea has a certain immediate appeal.)

Another bit of science fiction – as far as we can judge – was that offered by Plato concerning the lost continent of Atlantis, whose denizens were supposed to be highly cultured and whose civilization was, according to popular legend, sunk beneath the sea in a catastrophic grand finale of uncertain orchestration. Some said that Atlantis used to be beyond Gibraltar. It seems more likely nowadays that the story of Atlantis was pieced together from local legends surrounding the very real eruption of the volcanic Thera in about 1450 B.C., which destroyed a number of cities in Minoan Crete. It is known that this seismic event was of the magnitude of the nineteenth-century eruption of Krakatoa, which blew away four fifths of the biggest island in the strait between Java and Sumatra and threw up a cloud of dust and debris that colored sunsets all over the world for several years to come.

Of course, the submerged city is a common theme in the folklore of many countries: In Britanny and Cornwall, whose coastlines continue to submerge at an alarming rate, the oldest inhabitants can not only point to vast areas now under water that, fifty years ago, were dry or squishy land, but can also regale the passerby with many a story of cities that disappeared beneath the foaming brine. One tale in particular involves the retributive inundation of a city because of a bit of nastiness on the part of the local king's diabolical daughter. (The city in question was located, according to the Cornish folk, in Cardigan Bay and, according to their Breton cousins, in a spot called Ker-Ys.) One folklorist has wryly remarked that fairy cities are supposed to lie at the bottom of nearly every lake in Ireland. Like the tales of Atlantis, these legends are probably a healthy admixture of fact and fancy.

The Romans, who were not especially given to fancy, did not go in for exploration, either maritime or terrestrial. Their main interest was in winning, if not the hearts and minds of their inland neighbors, at least their peaceful subservience. Raiding coastlines or sailing off the edge of the earth featured not at all in the Roman game plans: The Romans preferred to do business, friendly or not, on land and in reasonably familiar territory. Their naval forays were chiefly military and by no means always successful, though their road-building techniques and the attendant use the Romans made of land-troop deployment strategies revealed an uncommon level of refinement.

After the fall of the Roman Empire, the Western world continued to stay pretty much at home, venturing no farther out into the ocean than to Iceland, and rarely that far, until the Vikings came along, sweeping south from Norway in successive waves from the middle of the eighth to the middle of the tenth century A.D. After repeated visits to the British Isles (where they were always coolly received), the Vikings moved on to Iceland where they found a few Irish monks but, apparently, nobody else in residence. From Iceland, hot-headed Eric the Red then sailed west to colonize Greenland on the other side of the ocean, managing to arrive there with fourteen of his twenty-five longboats still intact. From there, his son, Leif Ericson, explored the northeastern coast of America, possibly sailing as far south as Cape Cod but, encountering resistance from the local population, never planted a settlement. By the middle of the eleventh century, the whole operation had pretty much gone bust, and the Vikings sailed back home.

Exploration of the Atlantic and the Americas by European sailors was not to begin again in earnest until the end of the fifteenth century, with the wider distribution of maps and a whole slew of promotional literature favoring subsidy of the expensive expeditions facilitated by the invention of the printing press. Actually, the dissemination of maps remained controlled, as it has to this day, since much cartographic information was (and is still) considered too important strategically to share with one's enemies. Indeed, the Carthaginians used to keep their shipboard maps in lead cases, ready to throw overboard at the threat of capture.

Nevertheless, in spite of much information-hoarding, the world at large has gradually come to know a great deal about the ocean, matching or besting the Greeks' wildest imaginings. The Greeks were not too wide of the mark when they said that the lands of the known world were surrounded by ocean, since water does in fact cover three fourths of the earth's surface. Nor were they in error when they supposed that the ocean might be as deep as the mountains are high, for whole submarine mountain chains exist, some of whose peaks are higher from the sea floor than Everest is from sea level; and trenches near subductions, like the one off Puerto Rico, can be as deep as six miles or more. This particular abyss is populated by phosphorescent fish who live under such high pressure from the miles of water over their heads that they explode when brought to the surface by enterprising marine biologists.

As for the Atlantis myth or legend and the idea that islands can come and go, recent theories have arisen to make it all sound plausible: As the sea floor shifts and shakes because of continual movement of continental plates underlying both land and sea, fresh magma from beneath the world's underpinnings shoots up along the rifts, solidifies, and is eventually submerged again. Iceland, for example, is a volcanic creation of the Atlantic Ridge and may one day blow itself to smithereens and disappear in the deep.

Another Greek notion, that the world is surrounded by a vast riverlike body of water, is also not all that unreasonable or inaccurate. The Gulf Stream, which warms the coast of France and the British Isles, does travel in a more or less circular path from the Americas to Europe and back again at a steady rate of two or three miles per hour. European sailors were slow to discover this marvelous boon: John Cabot noted at one point in his voyage to the New World that the beer he had brought along all went bad because of a mysterious and unanticipated warmth below decks. And English sailors of the late eighteenth century, used to sailing the straight-line route to the colonies, scoffed at Benjamin Franklin's and Timothy Folger's 1770 map of the Gulf Stream, despite Franklin's admonition that contrary winds at the edge of the current could make a substantial difference – up to seventy miles a day – in the time it would take to sail between the Old World and the New if one made use of the current.

To the Greeks, no doubt, all of this would have seemed no more fantastic than Homer's tales of Scylla and Charybdis or the Symplegades, though two other uses of the letter *omega* in modern times might have left them scratching their heads: *omega* as the symbol in modern electrical theory for the eponymous Ohm, the unit of resistance; and *omega* as the symbol for resistance to the military draft.

DEAD LETTERS

Or

DIGAMMA DOESN'T LIVE

HERE ANYMORE

Everybody loses and forgets things. This is, after all, part of the human condition, as a visit to the railway station's lost and found or the post office's dead letter department will readily attest. Sometimes, the loss, say, of one's glasses, is purely accidental, the result of simple absent-mindedness. Sometimes loss or forgetting is ostensibly accidental but really in accord with subconscious wishes, as when you forget a dentist's appointment or lose the tickets to that concert that you didn't really want to go to anyway. And sometimes loss and forgetting are both intentional and institutionalized, as in the charming custom of the Mayans who used to sweep all of their worldly goods, so it is said, out the door on New Year's Day so as to make a clean start, a custom echoed in the Jewish practice of removing all leavened bread from the house just before Passover, and in other fits of spring cleaning the world over.

Attitudes toward loss and forgetfulness are sometimes reflected in the language itself. In Spanish, for example, you can say "*Se me perdió (olvidó) la llave*" for "I lost (forgot) the key," literally, "The key lost (forgot) itself on me." British English has "The key went missing" while some American dialects have "The key grew legs (and walked away)." In such cases, the blame is shifted away from the speaker and onto the inanimate object. Again compare: "It completely slipped my mind."

In borrowing a writing system, as the Greeks did from the Phoenicians, certain signs are bound to fall by the wayside. If the writing system is semi-ideographic, as were the prealphabetic scripts of the Near East, signs might be lost (and forgotten) either because the receiving language simply didn't have the words or concepts for which the borrowed signs might have stood or because some better way to represent certain words or ideas suggested itself. (One is reminded of the practice of assembling a model airplane kit by looking at the picture on the cover rather than at the directions, with the result that a few mysterious pieces may be left over.) Another possibility is that the word or concept for which the sign has been borrowed eventually disappears from the language, taking with it the sign itself.

In borrowing an alphabetic script from a language with a different sound system, letters are bound to be lost in like fashion. Similarly, a language may make temporary use of letters and then either lose the sounds for which they stood (and with them the letters) or else invent a better way to represent those sounds. English, for example, used to have two letters, *thorn* (Þ) and *edh* (ð), which stood for the initial, unvoiced sound in "thigh" and the voiced sound in "thy," respectively. These letters went by the boards when it was suggested that one could just as well use *h* after a *t* to represent these sounds, much in the same way as *h* was used after *c* to represent the initial and final sounds in "church" or, after *s*, the initial sound in "ship." (Actually, the English wound up trading greater phonetic accuracy for greater alphabetic economy by dropping *thorn* and *edh*, since the sounds these two letters represented were not and are not in fact the same, though both were and are of relatively low frequency of occurrence in the language.) It was, incidentally, at about this time that the increasingly evanescent *wh* sound, found in some dialects of English to this day in such words as "which" and "whale," came to be written *wh* instead of the earlier (and perhapes more revealing) *hw*.

The Greeks were great misplacers of orthographic gifts: Linear A and Linear B scripts attested in documents found in Crete were both lost and forgotten for centuries. In historical times, the Greeks lost three other letters that they had taken on a trial basis from the Phoenicians: *san, koppa,* and *digamma* (also known as *vau*).

The Semitic languages had a larger inventory of contrasting sibilant sounds than had Greek and, not surprisingly, a larger inventory of alphabetic signs for sibilants than the Greeks were ever able to use. They *did* find other uses for the Phoenician extras: Phoenician *zayin* and *shin* were taken over by the Greeks to represent their *z* or *dz* (*zeta*) and *s* (*sigma*) sounds. Phoenician *samekh* was used to represent *ks* in Western Greek. And *tsadeh* worked its way into and out of the Greek alphabet as *san*, being retained in the digraph *sanpi* (*sampi*), a combination of *san* and *pi*, for use in the alphabetical system of numeration that replaced the older acrophonic method.

The Greeks first represented numbers by using a single vertical slash for "one." Whether this convention was a throwback to the common tally-stick method of reckoning of many ancient peoples or had something to do with the stick-figure representation of the first letter of the Semitic alphabet, we cannot say, though it is worth mentioning that modern Arabic uses a single vertical slash for the first letter of its more or less alphabetic script and also for the number one. The number five was represented by the letter *pi*, the first letter of the word *pénte*, "five"; while *delta* stood for "ten" (*déka*); *eta*, in its original value of *h*, stood for "one hundred" (*hékaton*); and *chi* stood for "one thousand" (*chílioi*).

These letters, like their Roman numeral analogues, could be used to express numbers well, though numerical operations – addition, subtraction, and the precursors of multiplication and division – were bulky.

The Greeks then hit upon the idea of representing numbers by the use of alphabetic letters in a sort of *"alpha* equals one, *beta* equals two" system, with acute accents added to the right of each letter-number so that everybody would know numbers and not words were being represented. A primitive notion of place notation – ones, tens, hundreds, and so on – was expressed through this "new" system, which required the reinstitution of a number of previously "forgotten" letters – *sampi* (Ϡ), *koppa* (Ϙ), and *digamma* (F), for 900, 90, 6, respectively, though *digamma* was soon replaced by an alternate form of *sigma* (Ϛ).

The *san* of *sampi*, as we mentioned, had no real use in the representation of anything phonetic in Greek. The same may be said of *koppa*, representing the "back" or gutteral *k* sound of Phoenician and having no real analogue in Greek, though the name of the letter survives in Greek as *kappa*. The story of *digamma* (née *vau*) is a bit more complex. The Greeks had a *w* sound that the Phoenician *waw* was well-suited to represent. Eventually, however, this sound disappeared in Greek, though not before the Romans (via the Etruscans) had borrowed the letter to represent their *f* sound. When the sound disappeared in Greek, so did the need for this particular letter. Such is life and the vicissitudes of language.

Interestingly enough, the Greek phonetic inventory has come to include a similar sound once again in modern times, but now it is represented by the letter *beta*. The *b* sound is now represented by the digraph μβ (*mu* plus *beta*), just as plain *d* is now represented by νδ (*nu* plus *delta*), plain *delta* being reserved for representing an *eth* sound in the language. *Plus ça change, plus ça change.*

Bibliophilia

Millions of words have been written about the Greeks and their civilization, and about other ideas touched on in our book. Of necessity the following list is selective: We give (1) sources actually cited, (2) books we have found especially useful in the course of writing this one, even though we have not quoted directly from them, and (3) other books we feel are well worth looking into for further information, enlightenment, or just plain entertainment on the subjects central or tangential to this book – categories (1), (2), and (3) being by no means mutually exclusive.

Editions of many of the classics of Greek (and Latin) are available in facing English translation and original text in the Loeb Library series, published by Harvard University Press (Cambridge, Massachusetts). Most of these are also published in English translation by Penguin, based in Harmondsworth, Middlesex, England. Penguin has an office in New York City, and many titles are published simultaneously in England and the United States. For editions with original Greek text only, see the catalogue of Oxford University Press, though some are published in America as well, often heavily annotated and intended for use in schools. (See also the listings in *Books in Print* and the card catalogue at your local library.) Unless otherwise noted, the translations in the foregoing pages have been our own.

At the end of the general references, we have included a short list of dictionaries that we have found invaluable, not only for etymological information, but also for many enlightening bits of information about our subjects, illumination made the more delightful by the laconic style of the lexicographer.

Allen, H.; *A History of Wine* (London: 1961).

Apel, Willi; *The Harvard Dictionary of Music* (Cambridge, Mass.: 1969).

Barry, Sir Edward; *Observations . . . on the Wines of the Ancients* (London: 1775).

Becker, Thomas W.; *The Coin Makers* (New York City: 1969).

Benade, Arthur; *Horns, Strings and Harmony* (New York City: 1960).

Borgmann, D.; *Language on Vacation* (New York City: 1965).

Brill, Robert H.; "Ancient Glass," *Scientific American* (November 1963).

Brown, A. F.; *Normal and Reverse English Word List*, National Technical Information Service (Washington, D.C.: 1958).

Buck, Carl Darling; *Comparative Grammar of Greek and Latin* (Chicago: 1933).

Cajori, Florian; *A History of Mathematical Notation*, vol. I Chicago: 1928).

Campbell, L. B., ed.; *A Mirror for Magistrates* (Cambridge, England: 1938).

Chapin, Henry, and F. G. Walter Smith; *The Ocean River* (New York City: 1952).

Cottrell, Leonard; *The Bull of Minos* (London: 1955).

Culick, F. E. C.; "The Origins of the First Powered, Man-Carrying Airplane," *Scientific American* (July 1979).

Dawood, N. J., trans.; The Koran (Harmondsworth, Middlesex, England: 1956).

Diringer, David; *The Alphabet: A Key to the History of Mankind*, 2 vols. (New York City: 1968).

Einarson, Benedict; "Notes on the Development of the Greek Alphabet," *Classical Philology* (January 1967).

Field, Edward; *Eskimo Songs and Stories* (New York City: 1973).

Flood, Walter Edgar; *Scientific Words; Their Structure and Meaning* (New York City: 1960).

Freud, Sigmund; *A General Introduction to Psychoanalysis* (New York City: 1960).

————; *Moses and Monotheism* (New York City: 1939).

Gardner, Martin; *The Ambidextrous Universe* (New York City, 1964).

Gazzaniga, Michael S.; "The Split Brain in Man," *Scientific American* (August 1967).

Gesner, Konrad; *Curious Woodcuts of Fanciful and Real Beasts* (New York City: 1971).

Gilbert, Sir W. S.; *Plays and Poems*, edited by Deems Taylor (New York City: 1932).

Gimpel, Jean; *The Medieval Machine* (New York City: 1976).

Gloag, J.; *A Guide to Western Architecture* (New York City: 1958).

Gordon, Dr. Benjamin Lee; *Medicine throughout Antiquity* (Philadelphia: 1949).

Gordon, Cyrus; *Forgotten Scripts* (New York City: 1968).

————; *Ugarit and Minoan Crete* (New York City: 1966).

"Gossamer Wings," *Scientific American* (October 1977).

Graves, Robert; *The Greek Myths*, 2 vols. (Baltimore: 1955).

Grzimek, Bernhard, *Grzimek's Animal Life Encyclopedia*, vol. 13 (New York City: 1972).

Haining, Peter; *The Compleat Birdman* (New York City: 1976).

Harington, Sir John; *The Metamorphosis of Ajax*, edited by Elizabeth Story Donno (New York City: 1962).

Heath, Sir Thomas L., trans. and ed.; *The Thirteen Books of Euclid's Elements*, 3 vols. (New York City: 1956).

Hutchins, Carleen M., ed.; *The Physics of Music, Scientific American* offprints (San Francisco: 1978).

Huyghe, René, ed.; *The Larousse Encyclopedia of Byzantine and Medieval Art*, translated by Dennis Gilbert, Ilse Schreier, and Wendela Schurmann (London: 1963).

Jenkins, G. Kenneth; *Ancient Greek Coins* (London: 1972).

Jensen, Hans; *Sign, Symbol, and Script* (New York City: 1969).

Judge, Joseph; "Minoans and Mycenaeans," *National Geographic* (February 1978).

Kitto, H. D. F.; *The Greeks* (New York City: 1957).

Kuhn, Thomas; *The Copernican Revolution* (Cambridge, Mass.: 1957).

————; *The Structure of Scientific Revolutions* (Chicago: 1970).

Lacey, W. K.; *The Family in Classical Greece* (Ithaca, N.Y.: 1968).

Licht, Hans; *Sexual Life in Ancient Greece*, translated by J. H. Freese (London: 1932).

Lum, Peter; *Fabulous Beasts* (New York City: 1951).

Maloney, F. J.; *Glass in the Modern World* (New York City: 1968).

Mathew, Gervase; *Byzantine Aesthetics* (New York City: 1963).

McEvedy, Colin; *The Penguin Atlas of Ancient History* (Harmondsworth, Middlesex, England: 1967).

Menninger, Karl; *Number Words and Number Symbols* (Boston: 1969).

Menzel, Donald; *Our Sun* (Cambridge, Mass.: 1959).

Milner, Peter; *Physiological Psychology* (New York City: 1970).

Morgan, E. Victor; *A History of Money* (Baltimore: 1965).

Morris, Desmond, Peter Collett, Peter Marsh, and Marie O'Shaughnessy; *Gestures: Their Origins and Distribution* (New York City: 1979).

Nybakken, Oscar E.; *Greek and Latin in Scientific Terminology* (Ames, Iowa: 1959).

O'Brien, Flann; *The Third Policeman* (New York City: 1976).

Parker, E. N.; "The Sun," *Scientific American* (September 1975).

Payne, Robert; *The Gold of Troy* (New York City: 1958).

Pedersen, Holger; *Linguistic Science in the 19th Century*, translated by John Webster (Cambridge, Mass.: 1931).

"The Pharaoh's Wine Cellar," *Scientific American* (March 1978).

Pomeroy, Sarah; *Goddesses, Whores, Wives, and Slaves* (New York City: 1975).

Rahbar, Muhammad Daud, and Paul Alexander Humez; *The Urdu Letters of Mirzā Ghālib* (in preparation).

Roberts, W. R.; *Greek Rhetoric and Literary Criticism* (New York City: 1963).

Robinson, Cyril; *A History of Greece* (New York City: 1929).

Russell, Bertrand; *Autobiography*, vol. I (Boston: 1968).

Rybot, Doris; *It Began Before Noah* (London: 1972).

Sabine, Wallace Clement; *Collected Papers on Acoustics* (Cambridge, Mass.: 1922).

Sarton, George; *A History of Science*, 2 vols. (New York City: 1970).

Schmandt-Besserat, Denise; "The Earliest Precursor of Writing," *Scientific American* (June 1978).

Skrobucha, Heinz; *Introduction to Ikons* (Recklinghausen, W. Germany: 1961).

Smyth, Herbert Weir; *Greek Grammar*, revised by Gordon M. Messing (Cambridge, Mass.: 1963).

Soedel, Werner, and Vernard Foley; "Ancient Catapults," *Scientific American* (March 1979).

Somerset, Fitzroy Richard, 4th Baron Raglan; *The Hero: A Study in Tradition, Myth and Drama* (New York City: 1956).

Tunis, Edward; *Weapons: A Pictoral History* (New York City: 1954).

Walpole, A. S.; annotations to Greek text edition of Book I of Xenophon's *Anabasis* (New York City: 1963).

Weihaupt, J. G.; *Exploration of the Ocean* (New York City: 1979).

Weiss, G.; *The Book of Glass*, translated by J. Seligman (New York City: 1971).

Wheelwright, Philip, ed.; *The Pre-Socratics* (New York City: 1966).

Zall, P. M., ed.; *A Hundred Merry Tales* (Lincoln, Nebraska: 1963).

Zwicky, Arnold, et. al., eds.; *Studies Out In Left Field* (Edmonton, Alberta, Canada: 1971).

DICTIONARIES

The American Heritage Dictionary, edited by William Morris (Boston: 1969).

The Century Dictionary, edited by William Dwight Whitney (New York City: 1889).

Chambers's Biographical Dictionary (New York City: 1962).

Ernout, A., and A. Meillet; *Dictionnaire étymologique de la langue latine* (Paris: 1959).

Harper's Dictionary of Classical Literature and Antiquities (New York City: 1965).

Kaster, Joseph; *Putnam's Concise Mythological Dictionary* (New York City: 1963).

Liddell, Henry George, and Robert Scott; A *Greek-English Lexicon* (New York City: 1861).

The Oxford English Dictionary, Sir James Murray, general editor (London: 1933).

Index

A Paean

We could not have written this book without the active aid and encouragement of Warren Cowgill, Malcah Yaeger Dror, Ross Faneuf, Kathy Stavely Fitzgerald, Edward Goldfrank, Linda Hecker, David E. Humez, Jean M. Humez, Betsy Keithley, Dick McDonough, Susan Middleton, Morris Monsky, Bill Sarill, Rich Steiner, James Warren, and John Zarker. Their observations, suggestions, and inspirations have made a palpable difference. William B. Goodman, Dorian Hastings, Howard McMahon, Lucile McMahon, and Bob Nowicki were kind enough to slog through earlier drafts of the entire manuscript. Their careful reading and their tact in calling a number of infelicities and outright blunders to our attention have been greatly appreciated. Finally, we would like to thank David R. Godine for his unflagging support, for this has made the greatest difference of all.

ALPHA *to* OMEGA

---

has been set in Linotype Electra by Yankee Typesetters of Concord, New Hampshire. Designed by William Addison Dwiggins for the Mergenthaler Linotype Company and first made available in 1935, Electra is impossible to classify as either "modern" or "old-style." Not based on any historical model or reflecting any particular period or style, it is notable for its clean and elegant lines, its lack of contrast between the thick and thin elements that characterize most modern faces, and its freedom from all idiosyncrasies that catch the eye and interfere with reading. The display type in the book is handset Perpetua Titling, designed by Eric Gill, the eminent English sculptor and creator of letters with pen, chisel, and graver; it reflects his passion and talent for monumental inscriptional lettering. The Greek display type, designed in 1927 and intended to provide characters and symbols for mathematical setting, is Jan van Krimpen's Antigone Greek and Greek Open Capitals. Van Krimpen, like Dwiggins and Gill, was fundamentally a calligrapher and his chaste and fastidious faces are immediately identifiable as products of a European sensibility and a craftsman's understanding. Van Krimpen spent his entire working life at the distinguished Dutch printing firm of Joh. Enschedé en Zonen, under whose auspices a whole range of classic faces have been cut.

ALPHA TO OMEGA has been designed by Cynthia Krupat and printed on Monadnock Text, an entirely acid-free laid paper. Haddon Craftsmen, Scranton, Pennsylvania, was the printer and binder.